MW00582235

Calm Your Thoughts:

Stop Overthinking, Stop Stressing, Stop Spiraling, and Start Living

by Nick Trenton

www.NickTrenton.com

Table of Contents

Chapter 1. Introduction

With anxiety, life sometimes feels like a waking nightmare. It's like a veil of negativity is thrown over everything you think, feel, and do. Life can feel claustrophobic as more and more restrictions seem to interfere, making it hard to be spontaneous or relaxed. And the worst thing is you may not even understand *why* any of it is happening, nor can the people around you. It may seem like people explain away your anxiety as a bad attitude, to being oversensitive, or simply expect you to cheer up because they've thoughtfully explained all the reasons why your fears don't make any logical sense.

But it's never that simple, is it? In this book, we're taking a closer look at what anxiety is, how it works, and how you can learn to live a life that feels good to you despite experiencing anxiety. Stressful overthinking can feel like a trap, like something you can never escape or fix. But you can! If you're ready to make a genuine change, to take care of yourself, and to take some powerful first steps toward a low-anxiety life, then this book is a great place to start.

First things first: anxiety is a legitimate psychological phenomenon—you are not wrong or stupid or crazy. And you're not a bad person just because you haven't figured out how to free yourself from anxiety yet. I was diagnosed with GAD—Generalized Anxiety Disorder—when I was just eighteen, even though to be honest, the symptoms had been with me long before that. My life was ruled by FEAR. But today, I can honestly say that I have learned not to let anxiety control me, and one of the first steps to recovering was to let go of the habit of self-criticizing, self-blame, or feeling ashamed about how I was feeling.

Now, anxiety is not your fault, but it *is* your responsibility. What I mean is that I didn't choose to have anxiety—but I could always choose to do what it took to get out of its clutches. When I realized that I did have control over my life and that I had a say in how my life played out, I felt empowered to be better. It was (still is!) a long, personal, and challenging journey. But I don't regret a thing—except perhaps not believing in myself and starting sooner!

This book has been written for you if you have reached that point in your life where you feel like anxiety has you in its clutches and won't let go. Anxiety is strange—while you desperately try to keep control, you feel more powerless than ever and at the mercy of strong negative emotions that never seem to switch off. Many of us have a particular picture of what "anxiety" looks like, but this picture is bigger than you may realize.

Anxiety can play out in our work lives, causing us to feel self-doubt, imposter syndrome, or burnout. It can interfere with our relationships, coming between us and the people we love. It can wait for us in the wings, ready to sabotage our efforts and undermine our dreams and goals. It's there in our family life, with our friends, when we look in the mirror. Anxiety is in our thoughts, but it's also in how we feel and in every cell of our body. It's tight muscles, frazzled nerves, upset stomachs, sweaty palms, headaches, and allergies. It's lurking in our learned behaviors, every time we bite our nails, double check the front door, or turn down an invitation.

What I'm saying is, I don't quite know what anxiety looks like for you personally. I may talk about rumination, regret, low self-esteem, bad lifestyle habits, and rotten thinking patterns. Some of these things may apply to you and some less so. The anxiety tree has many branches, but I hope that as you read, you can recognize its roots in your own situation, even if it's not exactly the same as mine or the people I give as examples.

In this book, I want to teach you everything I've learned, and all the tips, tricks, techniques, and methods I've found to help you build self-compassion, upgrade thinking patterns, and take care of yourself, body and mind. The truth: it will take patience and stepping outside your comfort zone. But you *can* be a master of your lived experience, and you can absolutely discover joy and ease in your life again . . . I know you can because I did.

Like any change in life, it takes time and consistency. It takes courage. However deep the hole you're in, you can climb out one step at a time to live that full, rich, and fearless life you were always meant to be living. Let's dive in.

Why You Get Anxious

So, you've obviously asked yourself, *why me*? Why do I have to suffer anxiety?

The truth is that there is no single cause for anxiety, but many interrelated causes that all increase your risk or probability of experiencing overthinking, stress, and tension. Multiple causes can explain how some solutions (i.e. medication or CBT) work for some people, but not others. We all have our own predispositions, but we are also blessed, however, with protective factors and inner mental resources that help us push back against anxiety—when these inner resources are overwhelmed or depleted, that's when we have a hard time.

We'll look at the root causes of anxiety in more detail later on, but for now, here are just a few of the things that could be causing you to ruminate, worry, or overanalyze. (You'll notice that none of them are reasons to beat yourself up—remember, it's not your fault!)

- **A vicious cycle of learned behavior** – You know how it goes. You are anxious, and you feel bad about that. You avoid activities, which makes you feel worse, and develop anxiety *about* your anxiety . . . Anxiety is at heart a learned behavior and a coping mechanism (just not always the best one). But if you learned that behavior, then guess what? You can unlearn it.

- **A stressful lifestyle** – A punishing work schedule, chaotic home life, or grinding financial pressures will take their toll. Are you a workaholic with insomnia and bad eating habits? Are you in bad relationships, abusing substances, or dealing with crisis after crisis? It's no surprise you have anxiety.

- **Genes** – Yes, there is a hereditary component to anxiety. Having "anxiety genes" doesn't mean you will develop anxiety, only that you are more vulnerable to it. A tendency doesn't mean your fate is written in stone, though. What you inherit from your parents is a *potential range*— your lifestyle and choices determine where on that range you fall.

- **Abuse and trauma** – Whether that's childhood trauma, a discrete upsetting event, or simply the ongoing, low-grade trauma of daily life. Trauma is measured on a personal basis—there is no official subjective scale; it's all about what *you* find overwhelming and affecting, and feel unable to deal with. Anxiety can be the ongoing experience of carrying around unreleased or unprocessed trauma. Trauma can teach us maladaptive behavior patterns that help us cope in the short term but not so much in the longer term.

- **Life** – Life itself causes anxiety! Even if we're doing everything right,

13

simple everyday life can be stressful. Sad, upsetting, or disappointing experiences can worry us, naturally. A string of negative events can make you pessimistic or fearful, burning out your coping mechanisms. Being constantly in a physiological fight-or-flight mode drains your inner resources and leads you to panic and eventually shut down.

- **Poor physical health** – Your thoughts and feelings come from your brain, which is a part of your body. Body and mind are one interconnected entity. If you are unhealthy, it manifests in an altered neurochemical profile, hormonal imbalances, and a heightened biochemical stress response—and this feels like anxiety. But lifestyle and habit change is more effective at finding balance than merely taking medication for "chemical imbalance." Think of checking your thyroid, reducing substance use, or testing for deficiencies. Stress and anxiety are physiological as well as psychological—and if you're already in poor health, it's going to be much more difficult to deal with.

- **Dwelling on the past or worrying about the future** – This is a mental habit that takes you out of the living present and forces your attention on what cannot actually be changed, leading to anxiety and paralysis. Negative thought patterns like catastrophizing, ruminating, and blame are similarly disempowering. If we focus on things that we can literally do nothing about, we feel apathetic, powerless, resentful. It's a learned habit to force our focus on to those things we can change.

- **The environment** – We are all affected by the weather and the people and places we are surrounded with. Seasonal depression or being surrounded by others who are always in floods of anxiety can affect us deeply.

If you're like most people with anxiety, the cause of your anxiety is probably a combination of all the above, each connecting in complicated ways with one another. But this means that if we improve just one area, it usually has a knock-on effect, improving other areas too.

The Science Behind Your Brain's Negative Bias

So, you're in bed in the early hours and can't sleep. You keep replaying a painfully embarrassing moment in your mind when you said something stupid and everyone stared at you in horror. It doesn't matter that this event lasted four seconds and happened more than a decade ago—your brain is telling you that it's *absolutely crucial* that you mull over it this very instant and decide once and for all whether those people are still all friends with each other and have been secretly talking about you all this time, agreeing on what an idiot you are.

You've forgotten the compliments your coworker gave you earlier that day, the gift you received from your mom, and the smile from that stranger you passed on the bus. That's all gone. All you can see is the horrified looks on your friends' faces from deep in the past. Why?

The answer is that your brain has a built-in bias. To put it very simply, **your brain prioritizes negative information**. The so-called negativity bias is what it sounds like—we all have an automatic heightened sensitivity to negative, threatening, or unpleasant data. Dr. John Cacioppo conducted experiments where he showed people various images (neutral ones, positive ones, and negative ones) and looked at the electrical activity in the cerebral cortex. He found that the brain always responded with stronger electrical surges to negative images than to positive ones.

The theory goes that we evolved this tendency because it helped our ancestors to survive. Any negative stimulus in the environment could well signal a serious threat—so those of our ancestors who were ultra-tuned in to these signals could best evade them and have a survival advantage (i.e. you can thank your ancient grandparents for your pessimistic outlook!). Being quick to perceive positive information matters less, since it doesn't confer any extra survival advantage. But this mechanism does mean that we overfocus on bad news and tend to forget about good news.

This disproportionate emphasis on the negative means that even those of us with objectively good lives can still feel stressed and unhappy—some researchers suggest that we require a five-to-one ratio of good to bad (or higher!) to begin to perceive that good. For example, in a relationship, couples were more likely to rate themselves as overall satisfied if they had this ratio of good-to-bad experiences/feelings with their partner. However, it also explains how someone may not be tempted to stay with their partner if they had an even fifty-fifty split of negative and positive!

What can we infer about the negativity bias? Well, first, that suffering from anxiety is not some sign that your brain is broken or that you're doing something wrong. Rather, it's simply a case of your natural and inbuilt negativity bias working against you. If we hope to overcome anxiety, we'll need to **counter** this bias somehow and tip the scales back in the right direction.

It's All About Control

When you worry or overthink or ruminate over something, you already *know* that it isn't rational. After all, you can calmly tell yourself all the reasons you should stop thinking about something . . . but that doesn't mean you can. You might constantly seek reassurance from others, try to calm yourself down, and chew endlessly over the same ideas until you feel worn out and trapped, unable to just tear your thoughts away from your obsession. But you can't.

When you're trapped in a worry cycle that's been going on for a while, it can seem like a jumble of stressful chaos that makes no sense. But in its own way, it does make sense. There is a clear trigger, and that is a *lack of certainty*.

Let's look at an example. You're worried your girlfriend is thinking of breaking up with you. Something she said made you feel unsure, and now you can't stop thinking about it. You are in a state of psychological

19

arousal and feel unpleasantly uncertain. Your brain doesn't want to be in that state, so it basically reasons with itself, "I don't know what's happening here, so I need to gather more information. If I can do that, then I can find a rational solution, and then, I won't be worried anymore."

Sounds like a good idea, doesn't it?

So, you get to work analyzing. You think and think. You dream up scenarios, pick apart past events, and think about possible outcomes. You ask people or read articles online. You ask your girlfriend directly if she's going to break up with you, and when she says no, your discomfort somehow isn't soothed, and you start to do more "research"—could she be lying? Why would she lie and how would you know?

To soothe the feeling of uncertainty, your brain goes into analysis mode. But can you see how all this analysis is actually triggering more discomfort rather than soothing it? It's tricky because the rationale seems good on the surface. Weighing the facts in an analytical way often does soothe you—at least in the short term. The trouble is that once your brain finds what looks like a solution, your analyzing mind will find another problem:

"I asked her, and she said she was happy with our relationship."

"Yes, but she could be lying."

"But she's never lied to me before."

"That you know of. Maybe *everything* she's told you is a lie and she's so good at it, you can't tell."

"But then if she was unhappy, she would leave."

"Maybe she is going to leave. Maybe she's thinking about it right now . . ."

Your brain is trying to help, it really is, but it's making things worse. Recall what set this whole process off: the desire to avoid the sensation of uncertainty. The problem is not that we are not in control or feel uncertain. The problem is that we are trying to <u>avoid or escape</u> the feeling of not being in control or uncertain. So, in trying to avert short-term discomfort, we actually create long-term discomfort for ourselves.

The only way to stop anxiety at its source is to confront and face uncertainty and feeling out of control without experiencing it as something bad and unbearable—something that you need to run away from or protect against. You need to teach your brain that uncertainty is okay, not dangerous, and not a problem. You need to learn a new response—to no longer try to force control, but to practice acceptance instead.

Remember that with worry and rumination, all your "research" is actually attempting to answer a question that is fundamentally unanswerable. Think about it. Is there *anything* in life that is one hundred percent completely free of risk and which you have total and absolute control over? So, if you are worried about the plane crashing, your brain can rattle off at a thousand miles an hour doing probability calculations . . . or you can accept that sometimes, accidents do happen, that planes do crash, and that the second you step on board one, you are not in control of whether it does or doesn't. Read that again: no amount of rumination will give you any more control over a situation than you naturally do. It only gives you the *illusion* of being in control—and a whole lot of anxiety.

So, what causes a lot of anxiety? **We are trying to avoid uncertainty by overanalyzing.** But we don't have complete control over how the future will play out. You may feel like if you can just answer your "worry question" once and for all, that will satisfy you and you can finally drop your rumination, but be honest, has this ever actually happened to you? Has there ever been an answer that allows you to say, "Okay, fine, I'm happy with that," and stop worrying?

There is actually only one way out of this spiral, and that is not to try to gain control, but to give it up.

Instead of pushing against uncertainty, embrace it. Instead of trying to answer your worry question ("Does she still love me?" "Do I have cancer?" "Am I going to fail the exam tomorrow?"), deliberately practice leaving it unanswered. Don't research, don't Google, don't ask others, don't write a list, don't think about it. Tell yourself that analysis is *not* the solution, but really just more of the same problem.

This may feel like the last thing you want to do. You may be strongly tempted to panic, and your mind will keep returning to the unresolved problem, convinced that if you could just XYZ, then you could release the tension and be free. But it's a trap. If you can sit with the feelings of uncertainty for long enough, eventually your anxiety will lower on its own.

Returning to our example, perhaps you notice mounting feelings of panic and distrust as you worry if your girlfriend really loves you. But instead of boarding that anxiety train and getting carried away, you stop. You notice what you're doing. You notice your body, your tense shoulders, how your breath catches in your throat (more on body awareness later on). You notice that little voice in the back of your head saying, "You could check her phone? Maybe that will resolve the issue for you . . ."

You stop. You realize that you are avoiding discomfort. You take a deep breath and just

. . . let the discomfort be. You do a mindfulness exercise and distract yourself. You keep breathing without trying to control. To your surprise, within fifteen minutes, your mind has moved on and it genuinely doesn't seem to be the end of the world anymore that you cannot read your girlfriend's thoughts. In time, you develop something special: emotional resilience, i.e. *anti*-anxiety.

In the chapters that follow, I'll be sharing many different technique approaches designed to loosen anxiety's hold on your life. Most of them, however, will come back in some way to the cycle outlined above and attempt to teach you ways to control your emotions, halt overthinking, and become more mindful. Every human being must contend with uncertainty and doubt; those who suffer from anxiety may be encouraged to realize that they are not actually facing an extraordinarily high or dangerous level of uncertainty—only that their *response* is exaggerated. It can be a relief to see that you don't actually have to control the rest of the world around you, but merely yourself. This is the path of learning self-regulation, emotional mastery, and psychological resilience.

Chapter 2. Keeping Cool, Calm, and Collected

So, let's dive in. What does it really mean to be good at emotional self-regulation? Maybe you picture someone who is the proverbial "cool, calm, and collected," but how does someone *genuinely* find themselves in that state? To master anything, we need to understand it.

Regulate Emotions

Emotions are wonderful things. They add color and meaning and dimension to life. They make it all worth it.

But emotions are not always reliable. Recall that they are geared toward ensuring the survival of our species, but that's a goal with somewhat lesser priority in daily life. Like other parts of you, your emotions (anxiety included) evolved for a reason, but that doesn't mean we have to be at their mercy, especially given that modern life is so different from the one our brains evolved in. First, it's worth noting that emotions, including negative ones, are not a mistake or a problem. They're a normal, natural part of life, and we are not seeking to be free of them (does anybody *really* want to be an emotionless robot?).

We know that suppressing them is not the answer either and that you should allow yourself to feel even your darkest of feelings so that you can release them. After all, suppression and denial cause their own problems, and you probably already know that simply ignoring how you really feel does little to make it go away. So, a person who is a master of emotional regulation is *not* someone who experiences fewer or less intense emotions. They are in charge of their emotions, rather than the other way around.

There is a time and a place for expressing emotional needs, and sometimes you may just not be in the right situation to do so. Yes, you may feel positively filed with rage and anger, but if you're sitting in a church during a somber funeral service, for example, you simply have to manage that emotion rather than letting it run wild. Regulating your emotions means dealing with your emotional needs in a healthy and socially acceptable way—consciously and deliberately. This chapter will explain how you can release your emotions in ways that won't make you embark on a downward spiral.

Emotions are a constant part of our lives. Every minute of every day we will feel something, and our emotions can change in an instant. There are highs and lows that you experience every day, and how you deal with them can significantly affect your mental state and well-being. Our ability to regulate the vast number of emotions that we feel also affects how the people in our lives perceive us. It can be difficult when you are caught up in these moments to regulate your emotions and think of the consequences, but the more you do it, the more it becomes habitual.

The first and foremost way of thinking about emotional resilience and calm is the *react versus response* model. It is succinctly summed up in the image below:

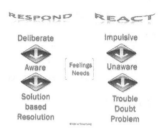

Overall, emotional regulation begins and ends with this image. To *react* to a situation means a complete lack of regulation because there is no thought. It is impulsive short-term thinking. If we touch a hot stove, we react by yanking our hand away as quickly as possible to avoid a burn. All we are focused on is immediate relief, and rational thought is not possible during this phase.

To *respond* is to take time to consider the alternatives and make a decision based on the information you have. It may not always be the right one, but you won't be acting on impulse or elevated emotions. This is where rational thought lives, and either healthy coping mechanisms can be utilized or the emotions are given time to process and freeze over. It isn't just about controlling what you feel, but also about thinking rationally about what the best course of action is. Focus less on your intense emotional impulses and more on desired outcomes and rational decisions.

This is obviously impossible in the case of the hot stove, but it's very, very rare that we are encountering the emotional equivalent of a hot stove. The problem is that we continually view any transgression as something that requires an immediate reaction, and this becomes hardcoded into our habits until we are a walking volcanic reaction (and not response). Thus, the important part to recognize here is that you are probably so used to reacting that this chain of events cannot be mentally separated for you.

For instance, when you wake up in the morning, you use the bathroom, brush your teeth, wash your face, and put your clothes on. Is it likely that you'll forget any of these elements? No—because just like your emotional reactions, they cannot be mentally separated from the trigger. They are linked in a way that is so natural now that you cannot imagine any other way.

Let's imagine an example of a fight between a couple about where to spend the holidays. In this situation, it may have been that you both wanted to spend the holidays with your own family and that they wanted you to spend it with theirs. A reaction to this might mean that you immediately discount the other person's opinions and assume that they want to control your actions or that your family doesn't matter. Without even thinking about the purpose and weight behind your partner's words, you simply begin to throw blame, feel anger, and then pick a fight about priorities. (Of course, there are some emotional needs being exposed here.)

Responding would be entirely different. The first step of responding is to take a moment to think and ask *why*. The answer may be that they haven't seen their family in a far longer time. What if they have a family member in ill health? What if they dislike your family, as your mother always lobs passive-aggressive statements about their weight? This brief pause of consideration allows you to understand the other person's perspective and allows a rational discussion where both people will be satisfied or, at the very least, a conclusion will be reached. Responding is almost never *easy*, but it is *simple*.

Differentiating between reacting and responding is the first step toward true emotional regulation and keeping even-keeled. It's the first place where self-awareness can be your best friend.

A Regulation Framework

After one or two instances where you've chosen the path of responding versus reacting, you may begin to see the value of keeping your emotions in check. It's one of the most difficult tasks in the world, especially if you don't have much practice with it. This is the first and arguably toughest step, and there isn't much I can tell you about it other than to breathe deeply, make sure not to act when your heart rate is elevated, insert as much time as possible between the external trigger and your response, and continue to ask yourself on a constant basis, "Why am I feeling this?"

Soon, you'll require a new set of tools for greater emotional control. You'll find that you are responding versus reacting, and yet your emotional state may not be upbeat or happy. You are still annoyed and peeved even though you haven't acted out. This is where a framework for emotional *regulation* comes in handy.

Of course, some emotional responses require no regulation—mostly positive ones. Laughing at a friend's joke or crying during a sad film are acceptable behaviors in their specific contexts. If an emotion is appropriate and helps you feel better, then there is no need to regulate.

For example, your impatience and anger at waiting in a long line. It might make you feel better, but it is neither appropriate nor productive. How can you regulate something like this by either expressing this frustration in alternative means or regaining your emotional composure? Stanford psychologist J.J. Gross came up with a five-step method for regulating emotion.

The first step is to select the situation.

This means that you should seek to avoid situations that trigger unwanted emotions in the first place whenever possible. If you have an allergy to peanuts, you can simply stay away from them.

Imagine that you have recently decided to partake in a marathon. You've been training hard, eating healthily, and increasing your endurance. However, maybe you find that you lose motivation when you see others at the gym and they seem to be running so much faster than you or lifting so much more than you. This is where you can employ this step. Maybe you will go for more runs outside instead of in the gym.

It doesn't mean that you are escaping your problems. It simply means that to keep your emotions up, you chose not to surround yourself with things that might bring you negativity. Remove yourself from dangerous situations so you don't have to regulate at all. You have more of a say than you think.

The next step is to modify the situation.

This is when you cannot employ step one. Let's say that you work late and choose not to run outside because it's cold and dark. You know that at the gym, you normally have feelings of inadequacy and you wish to reduce this. This is where you have to face the situation you have been trying to avoid, so you need to modify it to reduce its impact on you. You modify the situation to insulate your emotions by actively changing the terms for success. You alter your expectations to something that is more realistic and doesn't set you up for failure. Just because you can't go as fast as someone doesn't mean you can't run for as long. If you adjust the rules and make it so you are competing only with yourself, then you are in a can't-lose situation. After all, you are the one writing the rules for yourself—why do you need to be so strict and harsh?

The third step is to shift your focus.

When you can't avoid or modify a situation, you can always change what you focus your attention on. If you're upset by something, you fixate on it to your own detriment. Instead of being preoccupied by runners faster than you, shift your focus to the gym-goers who are much, much faster than you. You can also shift your focus to yourself and your own running—perhaps you aren't running so fast because you're always distracted and discouraged. Concentrate on improving yourself and reaching your own goals instead of beating someone else.

You don't need to compete with anyone but yourself. Whatever negative thoughts seem to be taking your attention, switch to positive ones. See the brighter side and try to feel gratitude for what you still have and others don't. It's quite difficult to feel both gratitude and emotional turmoil simultaneously.

Step four is to change your thoughts.

At the core of our deepest emotions are the beliefs that drive them. By knowing this, you can change your emotions by changing the beliefs that sustain them. Your negative belief is that everyone at the gym is judging you for your failures—therefore, your emotions will reflect that.

This is where you need to change your thoughts. To do this, think about how you view others at the gym. Most of the time, you don't really care what they do, or you think their performance is better than yours. By that reasoning, what if they feel the same about you? Believe that people don't judge and aren't even paying attention to you, and your emotions will follow and relax.

What is the evidence that your beliefs are true, and what is the evidence that they are not? If it helps, literally make a list and tally up the score.

The fifth and final step of emotion regulation, when all else fails, is to change your response.

This is true regulation. This is when no other steps of this process work and you find yourself feeling without limits. Maybe you feel utterly destroyed, decide to give up, and are very close to tears or rage. Take a deep breath to gather yourself, close your eyes, and pause. Gather your inner reserve and force yourself at least to change your facial expression and *keep it in*. You're still in react mode.

Obviously, you won't be able to. I did mention that emotional suppression was unhealthy, but this is different because you are trying to make it to the point where you can respond instead of react. When we can reflect a bit more, often we will find perspective and a different and healthier way to respond. By pausing in your tracks and taking a few moments to let them dwell on your emotions, you will find that you can actively regulate them.

Another similar model is called the STOPP Method, created by Carol Vivyan. STOPP stands for:

- Stop
  - simply pause and try not to let yourself be overcome by emotion
- Take a breath
  - breathe deeply to keep your heart rate in check, and notice your breathing in a conscious effort to keep it slow and measured
- Observe
  - ask what is going through your mind, determine where your focus lies, discover what you are reacting to, and try to name the feelings swirling through your brain
- Pull back for perspective
  - ask yourself what is really happening, try to incorporate different perspectives, understand how little it ultimately matters in your life, and remember to not instantly see disaster

- Practice what works
  - proceed with the best action you can take for the time being, remember your values, make sure you are responding rather than reacting, and focus on your main goals for the situation at hand

Remember that inserting a delay between our intense emotions and our responses is always the end goal.

None of the steps in these emotional regulation frameworks are easy. And at some point, the thrust of the next section, simply increasing your tolerance to emotional discomfort and anxiety becomes a necessary step toward resilience and calm. The more you can take, the less you need to regulate. You'll recognize some common elements from the regulation framework we've just discussed.

The ABC loop

Sometimes we find ourselves falling into a loop where we are simply in an autopilot state of acting and thinking, which will always lead to undesirable outcomes. Your feelings get hurt, you shout and react, and you compound your negative feelings with guilt and shame. Or you face a new and scary situation with panic and avoidance, instantly convincing yourself that you cannot possibly rise to meet those challenges. If we've been engaging with these patterns for a long time, we might even have convinced ourselves that overthinking, overanalyzing, and rumination are the best, most rational path forward. In fact, you might *think* you are engaging in the framework of emotional regulation, and you might think that you are responding rather than reacting. But how can you know for sure?

These automated actions are very difficult to see in the heat of the moment because we are so used to doing them without thinking. This is why building self-awareness and understanding the patterns of your thought and behavior are essential for emotional resilience. Without this, you will only be able to address the symptoms and not the cause.

There are a few tools for this, and they emulate talk therapy in some ways because they force you to really analyze your actions and answer questions that you'd rather not. You'll recognize a few elements of these tools from prior chapters, but there is always a different perspective in each new tool that can assist with self-awareness.

The ABC Loop is a classic behavioral therapy technique that considers all the elements that contribute to a behavior. It stands for antecedent (A), behavior (B), and consequence (C). The middle section, the behavior, is often called the behavior of interest, and the technique works by looking at the before and after to understand why the behavior in the middle occurred. It's also what you want to examine and regulate or control—hence, the increased scrutiny on it. In isolating these three elements, we can begin to understand what is actually happening in the external world and how it relates to the emotions we feel.

Let's begin with the antecedent. This is the environment, the events, or the circumstances preceding the behavior of interest. Anything that happens before the event that may contribute to the behavior would fall into this category. When identifying the antecedents, consider where and when they are occurring, during what activity, with whom they occurred, and what any others were doing at the time. Write down a mental snapshot of everything you can recall; you never know what might be pertinent to the ABC Loop.

For example, perhaps you are someone who finds yourself constantly arguing with your parents. You might realize that most of the time you don't even agree with what you're arguing with, but you do it anyway. You want to stop this behavior so you think about the last time it occurred. Set the scene first. In this situation—dinner at your parents' house, early afternoon—things were going fine, the television was playing, the topic of the future came up, and you were talking about your job and your career goals. This is the antecedent.

Then we move on to the behavior, which is the focus of this technique. This behavior can either be pivotal, which leads to further undesirable behaviors, or distracting, which can interfere with your own life or the lives of others. In this case, the behavior is uncontrollable anger, which is pivotal because it causes stress and irrationality in other parts of your life, too. It is important to describe the behavior in full when looking back in hindsight. There is some overreaction on your part, a complete lack of listening and validation on their part, and the feeling that you must make yourself heard. In this situation, there are raised voices, dramatic gestures, insults thrown, and intentionally vicious comments being said, most of which were irrelevant to the actual argument.

Last is the consequence of the behavior. This outcome is important because it is often one that reinforces the behavior. If the consequence is one that is genuinely undesirable, most unwanted behaviors will not be repeated, but if there is some sort of reward that is incidentally received, then the behavior will continue.

In this case, the outcome may be that one of your parents, usually your mother, leaves the room upset and the dinner is cut short, whereby you then go home. However, you might feel that you have "won" the encounter by making your mother back down, and this would be a positive reinforcement to continue engaging in this sort of behavior. But is it actually positive if everyone has been worked up to a frenzy and is feeling the adrenal residue of a loud argument? You got a little piece of satisfaction, but it's probably not a net positive interaction here.

Now comes the analysis of the ABC. The antecedent, as mentioned before, is the family dinner. It is important to mention the last thing to happen before the behavior. In this case, it was questions about career goals and aspirations. Already we have identified an important factor of the situation. Considering this is the last casual question before the argument, it is clear that this is the catalyst. If you are looking back at your own event and are able to identify the catalyst, consider why it affects you so much. Do you always react in the same way?

If you can identify what it is that catalyzes a behavior you want to stop, then you can focus on it and actively try to redirect your behavior when you encounter a similar situation again. This is where we also start to think about emotional triggers and needs. Why is this so triggering for you, and what need is it uncovering that isn't fulfilled? This doesn't happen with everyone, just your parents; why are they triggering you, and what emotional need is intensified with them specifically?

The next thing to observe is the behavior itself. In this case, it is uncontrollable yelling, but it can be a whole range of different ones. Think about why it is that you choose this behavior. In this case, maybe you feel as if you're not being heard. Maybe you want to exercise some control or authority or overcompensate because you are feeling cornered. Whatever the reasoning behind it, think about what purpose it serves. Usually, this is a coping or defense mechanism. But is it actually helping? Your purpose here is actually to make sure that your emotional need is either defended or fulfilled—is your behavior working toward that goal?

If not, is there another way to behave to get a better outcome with regard to your emotions? Even if it is something as simple as taking a moment to calm down, leaving the situation, or telling someone that you are not in an emotional state to continue, find a way to redirect your behavior so that you produce a different emotional outcome.

The last thing to consider is the consequence. If it is a recurring behavior, then that must mean you get some reward out of it. In this scenario, your mother has left the scene directly after the argument and you are forced to go home. Maybe this is exactly what you want—to spend less time with your parents. Maybe you just want them to support your career, and when it seems they aren't, then you don't wish to be there anymore. Maybe you want to score a "win" over them or be the last person standing and have the last word.

Have you learned anything from this experience, or is the consequence simply that you will double down on your behaviors from before? Do you feel compelled to change anything to make it so that your antecedent isn't triggered even worse next time and the behavior doesn't keep growing in proportion? An easy question to ask is the following: does the consequence make you feel good or bad?

So now consider the overall outcome of this event that we have analyzed with the ABC Loop. We can see that we are emotionally triggered by some combination of our parents and the topic of the future and that there is a particular emotional need or pain that comes out in this setting (antecedent). Next, we see that our behaviors are a somewhat unhealthy response to this emotional need and pain and aren't necessarily about the topic or setting by themselves (behavior). Finally, we observe that we've defended our emotional need and pain so hard that we cause turmoil in the relationship (consequence), and though this is a small victory for your emotional shields, it only makes the antecedent and behavior more likely to be amplified in the future.

How can you change this sequence of events to make sure it doesn't happen again in the future? It always starts with questioning yourself and asking why you feel such emotional pain—this is what leads to the behavior and then to the consequence, where the cycle repeats all over again. You can either cut off the conversation before the emotional pain reaches a boiling point, or you can make sure that the behavior is something that soothes you and helps you cope.

For instance, if all you want is to be supported in your decisions, have a conversation that deals with this and leave it when it doesn't. If there is something you don't want to discuss, tell your parents that there are things you would prefer to be off limits and you might discuss when you're ready; leave it if they keep pushing you.

The ABC Loop helps you understand how to cut the cycle of lack of emotional control, and it explains why things tend to get worse over time, not better. It gives you the exact blueprint for better emotional resilience and calm: avoid or alter situations that can turn into an antecedent, and attempt to choose healthier behaviors when you are triggered.

In the realm of anxiety and overthinking, the ABC model gives you something to hold on to when you may feel adrift in old patterns and unconscious mental habits. If you can recognize an anxiety trigger (for example, being evaluated by someone in a position of power) and know that it tends to elicit a certain behavior from you (panic, avoidance, a spiral of negative self-talk), then you can take steps to avoid the usual consequences (a panic attack or self-sabotaging at work). The ABC loop gives the opportunity to step *outside* of the loop rather than get tangled in it. You can switch from unconsciously reacting to deliberately responding. In other words, once are aware of what is happening, you suddenly have something special: a choice.

Emotional Dashboarding

We've seen that our brain has a natural, inbuilt, and inherited tendency to focus on the negative, and that anxiety and overthinking come from our desire to control what is not strictly under our control. But when we can become conscious of these patterns, we have the chance to respond with deliberation and agency, rather than react blindly.

Emotional dashboarding is a similar process to the ABC Loop and is another way of helping you cultivate more conscious awareness and control over your anxiety. It also encourages stepping back from a situation to review your actions and reactions to break into your autopilot. While the introspective approach of emotional dashboarding is the same as the ABC Loop, there are a couple more incremental steps:

SITUATION/ FACTS	THOUGHTS	EMOTIONS	BODILY SENSATIONS	IMPULSES/ ACTIONS
Example: Project due tomorrow	*"I don't feel like doing this." "I shouldn't have to."*	*Sadness, boredom, irritation*	*Heaviness, fatigue*	*Go to sleep, eat, space out*

Situation. Jot down the literal facts of the situation—details that couldn't be argued

52

by any observer. This means leaving out opinions and existing prejudice or bias. This will help you understand the circumstances around your anxiety, overthinking, or emotional outbursts.

o A project is due tomorrow.
o Your spouse's family is arriving for the holidays.
o You're assigned a new supervisor.
o You've moved to a new place after a breakup and are invited to a party.

o Be very careful to be honest and neutral here—no interpretation, judgment, or clinging, just the facts. In a way, you are seeing the layout of the situation *without* your emotional engagement in it. Set the stage, so to speak.

Thoughts. Recall the personal interpretations and thoughts that went through your mind when the first feelings of distress or avoidance came up. These are the beliefs and thoughts that are triggered by external events. Often, these are far more volatile and violent than the following examples because they lead directly to the next step of emotions and emotional needs and pain. Really try to articulate your inner monologue, as it can literally tell you everything you need to know about your mental and emotional state.

- o "I don't feel like doing this"; "I shouldn't have to."
- o "Last year they seemed judgmental about the appearance of our house."
- o "I've heard bad things about this person from people who've worked under him."
- o "I'm not sure I'm ready to mingle with strangers in an unfamiliar place."

- o Really dig into these if you can. Put words to the sensations and beliefs. It might not seem like it, but every action is preceded by a belief or thought that is itself triggered by the circumstance. Slow your inner dialogue down to see what stories and beliefs are running through it.

Emotions. Take a measure of the feelings you experienced during this conflict using only single emotion words. For our purposes, be sure to also think about the emotional need or pain that is being invoked. Make the connection from the external actions to your thoughts and to your emotions. See them as a continual cycle, a cycle that we are trying to understand and ultimately cut in favor of something healthier or happier.

o sadness, boredom, irritation
o resentment, disfavor, annoyance
o anxiety, fear, concern
o dejection, tension, uneasiness

When naming your reactions, ask yourself three times why these emotions came up. The repetition of the question will encourage you to go as deep as possible and get to the root of the problem. In the first example, what mental picture caused the sadness about the late project—fear that it won't be good enough? Is the boredom because you feel it's a routine that keeps recurring? Are you irritated because there was a social event you would rather have done tonight?

Bodily sensations. Mark down the physical sensations you felt when experiencing the conflict. These can add clarity to your emotions, because while we can lie to ourselves, our bodies can only react and will almost always tell the truth.

o heaviness, fatigue
o stomach upset, headache
o shoulder tension, increased heartbeat
o lightness in head, slight tremors in hands

Be as literal as possible in describing bodily sensations. Avoid metaphors like: "My heart was jumping out of my chest." Instead, say, "I felt my heartbeat accelerating." Sometimes our bodies know something far sooner than our brains can register. Anxiety in particular is not just a mental phenomenon, but a complete bodily experience. Your anxious thoughts and feelings are the final and most obvious manifestation of the anxiety, but what does this anxiety look like in your gut? In your chest or on your skin?

Impulses/actions. Write down your first instincts of what you wanted to do to relieve or avoid the conflict—things that made you feel good, distracted you, or minimized your attention to the preceding sensations. If these are relatively benign or healthy, that's a good thing. However, if your first impulses are to retreat or get lost in overanalysis, then you know a chord has been struck. Something is happening within you, and it is being demonstrated through your actions. You are likely in the midst of an unconscious, repeating loop.

○ go to sleep, eat, space out
○ watch TV, surf online
○ do "busy" work, make phone calls, scream a little bit
○ drink alcohol, walk outside

Like the ABC Loop, the practice of emotional dashboarding produces a sequence of events that can be broken down and assessed like a fictional story. *Why did this happen, how can we prevent it, and what elements seem to be your downfall?* The dashboard adds a few internal elements—internal conflicts and physical sensations—that play the same role that "motivation" serves in fiction. Recognizing those alterations in your feelings and thoughts can help you identify them when they come up again.

This all may seem rather complicated, especially when anxiety seems lightning fast and irresistible in the moment. But just remember that you are *not* at the mercy of your anxiety, unless you agree to be. You can always stop and break down your experiences and work through them, consciously and on your own terms. Break it down:

- Situation
- Thoughts
- Emotions
- Bodily sensations
- Impulses/actions

At first, it may work to literally write all this down in a notebook, but in time, you can do this more automatically and see more easily how all the above blend into one another. Is the ABC model or the "dashboarding" approach better? In truth, they are variations of the same exercise.

One method may seem more appropriate than the other, depending on your circumstances. You may want to use the ABC Loop when initially coming across a conflict, then the dashboard if it happens again or gets worse. If you notice a new pattern of anxiety emerging around your behavior with your work supervisor, for example, you may choose to run an ABC Loop first. If you keep having the same problems (for example, you keep avoiding, procrastinating, or self-sabotaging because of anxiety), you might want to run through the dashboard to see if you can gather additional insight about your deeper thoughts and feelings behind the behavior.

It may simply be easier or more efficient just to execute an ABC Loop. Or perhaps your anxiety is so acute that you'd rather run the emotional dashboard. With honest self-inquiry, either method can help you make headway in discovering patterns and identifying troubling behaviors to change.

But with both, progress starts with awareness—any time we can wake up and take conscious control, we make strides in combatting anxious overthinking.

Worry Postponement

One amazing (and amazingly simple) technique for putting the brakes on the anxiety spiral is called worry postponement. In fact, you don't even need to suffer from anxiety to benefit from using it—it's a great all-around stress management technique. A little like making a stress budget.

Anxious and worried thoughts are kind of sticky. They have an intrusive quality. Once a threatening or negative thought pops into your head, it seems hard to shift or ignore. You can quickly get distracted since your brain thinks, "Oh, here's what I *really* should be paying attention to!" and just like that, your attention and focus is pulled away from the present moment.

So, what's really happening is that worries are controlling you rather than you controlling them. A stressful thought comes along and cracks the whip, and you instantly obey. The mistake we make is to think that if a negative thought comes along, there is no other option but to focus on it. Remember our brain's negativity bias and our information processing software that literally evolved to amplify bad news? It tells us that the threatening and scary thing always takes precedence.

Now, if the worry is, "I wonder whether that tiger in front of me is going to try to eat me," then obviously, prioritize that. But usually the worry is something like, "I wonder if Jenny thinks my presentation sucks," or, "What if identity thieves have gone through my trash and discovered that journal I threw out by accident, and now everyone at the FBI knows my terrible secrets?" In other words, we give these thoughts priority when we really, really shouldn't.

Worry postponement isn't saying you're going to completely eradicate worries (yes, we all have them, even non-anxious people). It's just saying you're going to put worries in their proper place. Rather than jumping to attention every time some anxiety idea pops into your head, you make it wait. *You* are in charge of where your conscious awareness goes. You don't allow just anything to distract you or disrupt your focus.

Worry postponement is exactly what it sounds like—a deliberate choice to *put off* worrying for another time. This is different from saying you won't worry. This is more about taking control and managing your worry, proactively deciding how much of an impact you want it to have on your life. In the moment, worry can seem so urgent and all-important. It can seem non-negotiable that you turn every fiber of your being toward those thoughts and feelings. But actually, you have a choice.

Worry postponement can be done in a few different ways, but it's all about setting deliberate and conscious limits to worry. Like drawing a little fence around it.

One method is to limit the time period when you worry. For example, you get into bed at night and prepare to sleep, but your brain instantly switches into worry mode and brings up a thousand things it wants to stew over. You tell yourself, "That's fine. I'm allowed to worry about that, and I will. But I won't do it *now*. I'll schedule a specific time to worry about this later. Let's say, tomorrow at 10:00 a.m. Before that period, I won't spend a single second thinking about any of this."

And then you do that. If your mind wanders over to those ultra-important, life-or-death thoughts, you can confidently tell yourself that it's fine, you'll think about it, just not now. Chances are, the worries are not all that time sensitive and can wait. In fact, you'll be fresher in the morning and can bring your full brain to the task, if you even still want to. Tell yourself you have already done everything you need to do, the worrying is ticked off the list, and there is nothing outstanding for you to do right now. Just sleep.

An alternative is to put limits on the duration of worry. So, you get up in your bed and tell yourself, "Right, you want to worry? Okay, let's worry. But we are only doing this for *five minutes*, and then we're going to sleep." Set a timer, worry your heart out, and then stop. You may notice a few things with either of these techniques.

The first is that if you delay the worry, you often don't want to do it later anyway. The second is that even when you do permit yourself some worry time, you'll often notice that your anxiety levels are exactly the same before the worry and after. Meaning, the worry time did precisely zero to help. In either case, you are limiting and managing the effect that worry has on you and teaching yourself that you have a choice and are not at the mercy of distracting, intrusive thoughts.

To practice this technique needs preparation and practice. Set a time everyday when you purposefully worry. Pick a time when you won't be disturbed, and when you're likely to be in your best frame of mind. Experiment a little and don't be afraid to try a few different things before it feels right.

I hear what you're thinking, though. Maybe you're wondering, "Sure, sounds good, but what if this time I really *do* need to worry about something? What if this time it's serious?"

Well, let's play devil's advocate and imagine that occasionally, our worries and fears and ruminations actually are very important and need to be considered immediately. What we need is a method for distinguishing between those situations and simple overthinking. We can ask ourselves the question: **is this worry a 1) genuine problem that 2) I can do something about right now?**

Be honest. The problem has to be both objectively critical, but also actionable in that very moment. Let's say there's a pressing work matter that's eating you up inside. It is indeed a real problem, but let's say it's late at night and the one person you need to speak to is unavailable until morning. So, the problem is genuine but you cannot do anything about it now. Let's say your child has a fever but is otherwise fine, but you could possibly rush them to the emergency room to be looked at. This is a problem that can be acted on, but it isn't that genuine a problem. Finally, imagine you're worried a recent client is going to leave you a bad review. In reality, this is not really a serious problem (no business ever failed on the back of a single bad review), *and* there's nothing you can do about it right now.

But what if it is a serious problem and you can act right now? Then act.

But act—don't worry. Worry and overthinking are useless, particularly when appropriate action is what's called for. Here, you need to worry even less, since having a calm, clear mind is what will help you see the solution most quickly. Unless your anxious thought is genuinely serious and you can do something sensible in the moment, then postpone it. Make the call in the morning, sort it out later, or just drop it for the time being.

Once you've decided that something is not worth worrying about, be ruthless. Imagine your mind is a dog on a leash and keep pulling it back to the present. This is easiest to do if you engage all five of your senses to anchor you in the real, present moment. Examine your environment to see if you can list three sights, three sounds, three smells, and so on.

When worry time comes, notice if the urgency seems diminished somehow. Remind yourself that what once seemed urgent doesn't stay that way. Look with fresh eyes on concerns and anxieties. Go into problem solving mode and see if committing to taking useful action reduces your anxiety. Sometimes, the best thing you can do for a worry is to pull it into the real world, make it a practical problem, then act on it.

Using the Five WHYS

Sometimes overthinking takes a vague, nebulous form, jumping from one thing to the next. Other times, you're anxious because of something you can definitely point to—for example, a difficult decision you have to make or a problem you have to solve. Sakichi Toyota's technique of the "five whys" is a useful framework to guide your thinking into something useful and away from stressful rumination.

Start by defining the problem. What is the issue, exactly? Let's say your dog is barking and acting threateningly to the neighbors, aggravating them, and leading to them threatening a call to the authorities. They tell you in no uncertain terms: you need to *do* something. If you're ruled by anxiety, you may start to go down a spiral—what are you going to do? Are they going to complain and the SPCA take your dog away? Do they hate you now? Is everyone in the neighborhood similarly angry?

But slow down and work your way through the questions. Ask yourself, **why is this happening?** Why is your dog barking and harassing the neighbors?

"My dog is still young and an energetic breed. During the days, she gets bored, and I think she barks because she's restless. She doesn't mean any harm!"

Now ask the question again: **Why is that?**

"Well, I guess she's bored because she hasn't had her walk yet. I only walk her in the evenings."

Why is that?

"That's the most convenient time. I can't do it in the mornings."

Why is that?

"Because of my new shift pattern. I need to get to work really early."

Why is that?

"Because we've retrenched half our team and I'm picking up all the slack!"

And there, according to the method, is your root cause. It seems like a stretch to link your grouchy neighbors with recent changes at work, but there you go. Now, you have a choice. You can take steps to look for better work that doesn't eat up all your time, or arrange for a different shift pattern. That way you can walk your dog, and then she won't bark as much. Or, you could pay a dog walker.

Granted, this is a very simplistic example. You'll come up with different answers for bigger and more complex problems. Occasionally, more than five questions may be needed, or fewer. You might use this technique to quickly decide what to do about a minor annoyance (you're double booked, now what?) or major life decisions or dilemmas (you're completely restructuring your business after a massive downscaling . . .).

If your worry is aimless and formless, this technique may not be appropriate, but if your worry is spiraling out of control specifically because you're facing big problems and decisions, take a deep breath and allow this method to cut through the clutter for you. Keep asking why, identify the root cause, and then you are empowered to act to change that root cause.

What you'll notice about this technique is that you need to start out with the correct framing of the problem. If you can and want to, ask others for their input to identify any personal blind spots that may be influencing you. For bigger issues, don't rush your answers. Really pretend you know nothing and look at things with a fresh perspective. Don't answer what you think you *should* answer. If you want to arrive at a truly insightful result, you need to give meaningful answers along the way.

Here's an example of a bigger issue:

Problem: I can't seem to sell my house and it's stressing me out. What's wrong with people?

Why is that happening?

People are looking at the online listing, but nobody is booking viewings.

Why would people look without booking a viewing?

Maybe the house is nice but the price is too high.

Why would the price be too high?

Because I paid a lot for this house myself, and I'm terrified of losing some of that equity. So I've priced it so I make a small profit.

Why do you need to make a profit?

Uhhh ... I guess because I feel like I ought to sell it for more than I bought it for. If I'm honest, I think I paid too much.

Why did you pay so much for this house?

It was my first house and I was anxious I'd miss out.

Now look at the problem again. Without delving deeply, the problem *seems* like, "What's wrong with people?" but on closer inspection, the real impediment to a house sale is, funnily enough, psychological resistance rooted in anxiety. By following the questions, though, you can see for yourself that regret about paying too much in the past and resistance to losing any more money is preventing you from selling *now*.

Instead of ruminating over it endlessly ("Why, why, why don't people want to buy my house?"), you can simply take action that will address the root cause. You might work toward accepting that you made a poor financial decision and come to terms with the fact that you might lose some money. This means you can finally lower the price and, probably, sell the house.

Be careful, though. The five whys are only useful if your worries have some genuine basis in reality, i.e. there is a real crisis they center around. You want to cut down on confusion, not encourage it. If you notice these five questions spur you to endless rumination and "research," then stop. You'll know the method isn't working for you if you arrive at your final answer and still feel anxious and unsettled. Your best bet in that case is to stop, distract yourself, or engage in worry postponement until the anxiety subsides.

Summary

- Tackling anxiety comes down to the learned skill of emotional regulation. Rather than deny or squash down our natural emotions, we learn to *manage* them consciously and deliberately. We do this by becoming **responsive** rather than **reactive**.

- Becoming responsive is about pausing before we act in a situation, practicing impulse control, looking at our own motivations, beliefs, and thoughts, and finding healthy solutions to problems that go beyond anxious overthinking.

- One way to be more responsive is to dissect situations in the ABC framework—antecedent, behavior, and consequence. We need to examine what precedes and what follows anxious behavior, and then work around it. Building self-awareness of your habitual patterns takes time and is seldom caught in the heat of the moment. But by engineering our triggers and outcomes, we can take control of our anxious behavior and change it.

- Emotional dashboarding is a similar approach designed to introduce more conscious awareness and reduce reactivity.

- We carefully analyze the factual situation, our emerging thoughts and beliefs in that situation, our resulting emotions, our physical sensations, and the impulses or actions that all of this inspires (i.e. anxious overthinking). When we are aware of all the precipitating factors, we can step in and avert falling into the anxiety spiral.

- Worry postponement is a very direct and effective way of interrupting anxiety spirals. When you recognize yourself beginning to feel anxious, deliberately schedule a discrete time in the future to worry instead, and then continually bring your mind to the present. We can seldom eliminate worry from our lives, but we *can* consciously limit its time of onset and the duration.

- Finally, the five whys is a method that can help you put definite and useful shape to vague worries and overanalysis. If you're dealing with a real problem or crisis, the five whys can help. Define the problem and then ask what caused it—repeating the why question five times to arrive at the real root cause, which you can then act on.
- Avoid this method if your anxieties are not attached to any real dilemma or decision. The questions are designed to elevate overthinking into clarity and problem solving—not more overthinking!

Chapter 3. Debugging the Machine

Your brain is not an inescapable prison designed to torture you, while you have no control over how you think or feel. It's a tool—a machine—that you can use as you see fit. One of the biggest reasons that anxiety takes a hold on us is actually a little ironic—in believing that anxiety itself is something to avoid or feel bad about, we trap ourselves in worry spirals. We've talked about emotional regulation, but beneath this skill is a fundamental mindset shift, i.e. the idea that negative emotions are not the end of the world, they are not unbearable, and that we are more than capable of weathering them.

In this chapter, we'll be looking more closely at the characteristics and mindsets of people who are not naturally anxious. Their worldviews, attitudes, and perspectives on life give them an immunity to distress. Importantly, they don't experience any less stress than you or I do—but they interpret it differently and give it a different meaning. Once you're practicing becoming less reactive and mastering your own emotions using something like the ABC framework, you will naturally start to experience a shift in perspective.

You will start to see distress, discomfort, and uncertainty as a normal part of being alive—and you will also start to take your skillful management and acceptance of these feelings as a given!

Distress Tolerance

Distress is a natural part of life. Every person at some point or another needs to face discomfort and anxiety; it's not a question of whether you'll have to endure it, but *when*. Fortunately, emotional resilience is something that can be learned and cultivated with a plan and frequent practice. We can all learn to lower the stress in our lives and remove triggers, yes, but we can also do a lot to elevate our own resilience and mental toughness so we're simply not as bothered anymore!

While many might choose to focus on avoiding emotional discomfort or arranging a life where they don't have to experience it, a truly resilient person trusts in their own ability to withstand distress and not just survive, but thrive. Most importantly, having a higher degree of distress tolerance makes you hardier; you won't even have to use coping or self-awareness tools as often, because you simply won't reach those heightened negative emotions as frequently. Greater tolerance to distress and anxiety can be mastered over time using just a few simple steps.

Step 1: Identify Your Triggers

It always goes back to the triggers, doesn't it? Whether this is a particular situation, event, person, words, memories, thoughts, body sensations, sounds, or images, a trigger is like a bell that starts us off down the path of distress. Sometimes, a pattern of distress can happen swiftly and without our conscious awareness, leaving us clueless as to why we're suddenly upset. One moment you're feeling fine and going about your day, and the next you feel the escalating sense of panic, anger, or sadness. But what happened?

If you look closely, you can always identify the precise stimulus that caused your emotional response. It's tempting to think that emotional control and mastery is all about wrestling emotions once they're already in full swing. But with practice, you can start to see the small seeds of distress *before* they sprout into overwhelming emotion that's hard to get a grip on.

Imagine a woman heads home for the Christmas holidays to be with her family. She starts the visit feeling calm and balanced and has told herself that she'll keep her cool even though her family is notorious for heated arguments and upsets during the holidays. Despite feeling okay for a while, she soon notices her mother's messy kitchen and feels herself getting agitated at how chaotic the food preparation is, with everyone talking over each other and weighing in on how best to prepare the Christmas meal. Then she notices she's starting to feel a bit physically warm, given that the fire is crackling away in the next room and several people in warm jumpers are bustling in and out of the kitchen. Finally, her father makes a hurtful comment about the way she is chopping onions, and like a dam breaking, she suddenly feels extremely angry and upset and snaps at everyone. In other words, she's distressed.

Rewind the situation and it's clear that there are several triggers instigating these feelings of anger and unhappiness. These are both external (noise and bustle, untidiness, criticism from loved ones) and internal (the feeling of chaos and stress, feeling too warm, not feeling good enough, or perhaps recalling negative memories and associations from childhood).

Triggers can be literally anything. Anniversaries, money problems, arguing with your family or spouse, workplace conflict, going to the doctor, taking an exam, falling ill, having to compete with others, thinking about the future, being rejected . . . The list goes on and on.

How do you find out what your *own* triggers are? A good way to think about this is to look at past behavior and try to understand what's reliably caused distress for you before. This takes a degree of awareness in the moment, but can you notice any patterns in what occurs immediately before you become emotionally overwhelmed?

The great thing about becoming aware of your triggers is that when they occur, they give you an opportunity to stop and take notice of what is happening. This gives you the option to step in and take action before becoming overwhelmed with strong emotions.

Step 2: Pay Attention to Your Warning Signs

Of course, a trigger is just a trigger—it's our response to it that makes all the difference. A warning sign can be thought of as any indication that you are having trouble dealing with some emotional distress. Again, these can be thoughts, emotions, or the urge to behave in a particular way. They indicate that distress is underway and that you are dealing with strong unpleasant emotions.

What could happen at this point is that you resort to "escape methods" to try to avoid the distress. We've already discussed the need to quell uncertainty by overthinking or ruminating in a bid to gain more control, but avoidance and escape can take many different forms. These kinds of behaviors can be as varied as the triggers that they're designed to avoid. In addition to overthinking, they can include seeking assurance, distracting yourself, resorting to substances or overeating, oversleeping, or simply avoiding the stressful situation completely.

In the example of the woman above, the mounting emotional stress she experienced leads to a very clear warning sign: snapping at the people in the kitchen with her. Whereas the triggers might have been small bells, warning signs are more like blaring fire alarms. Warning signs are not just actions, however. They can be thoughts (for example, "I can't do this," or, "I'm a failure") or feelings (for example, irritation, panic, depression, shame, or jealousy) or even physical body sensations (for example, fatigue, shaking, a knot in the stomach, tension, or tearfulness).

It can be difficult to clearly see distress as it unfolds in the moment, precisely because distress is so unpleasant and we're often seeking ways to avoid it at all costs. That's why the regular practice of distress tolerance will sharpen your ability to zoom in on your unique triggers and exactly how they affect you.

Step 3: Forego Your Escape Mechanism and do the Opposite

Step 3 is where your distress tolerance plan really comes to life. Being triggered and experiencing overwhelming emotional, mental, and physical sensations can force us down the path of automatic habits designed to make us feel better. However, *escape behaviors* seldom give us the opportunity to develop resilience and grow as people, and frequently the escape behaviors themselves are harmful to us. It's because we are still operating under the core belief: *this is unbearable; I can't cope.*

The ABC model, worry postponement, or emotional dashboarding are all ways to gain awareness of what's going on, and using them wiggle conditions a little so there is less anxiety. But if we want to develop *resilience*, we can also choose to stay with a sensation instead.

For the woman in our example, snapping at family members is only likely to put them on edge and in turn feed the chaos and stress in the kitchen, unintentionally making matters worse. Other escape behaviors can be even more damaging—for example, binge-eating, alcohol abuse, or avoiding doing tasks at work that will only become worse with procrastination.

Though escape behaviors feel irresistible in the moment, and they may sincerely feel like our only solution at times, they are not ultimately adaptive and come from a place of avoidance, weakness, denial, and escape rather than confidence and strength to deal with what life throws our way.

How do you know what your escape behaviors are? This part of the process might be the easiest to identify since they'll be those actions you feel strongly compelled to do when in the thick of an overwhelming emotional reaction. Many people get intense cravings for sweet things after an upsetting argument, or feel compelled to get up and leave the room if the situation feels utterly hopeless and overpowering. Look closely at those behaviors you feel unable to resist when emotionally overwhelmed, and you'll likely learn something about your escape patterns.

The trick is then to deliberately and consciously commit to doing the opposite of that behavior, which invariably means to seek calm, not escape, and remain in the situation and emotion.

In a way, you are facilitating your own exposure therapy.

Triggers and warning signs are invitations to become aware in the moment and make the (admittedly difficult!) choice to take a different path. Luckily, this gets easier and easier the more you practice it. You might, for example, choose to quietly tell yourself, "I will stay with my feelings right now instead of trying to avoid them." You can silently say this sentence to yourself again and again in your mind, say it out loud, write it out in a journal, or even share your sentiment with someone close. The point is to bring your actions out into the open and convert an old automatic habit into conscious action that you have a choice in.

Knowing what your triggers and warning signs are ahead of time can help immensely with this. If you know that you are prone to thinking thoughts like, "This is unbearable," and resorting to self-harm to distract yourself, you may choose to instead recite a little mantra to yourself: "I *can* bear this. I am choosing to stay with my feelings and not escape them."

Step 4: Accept Your Distress and Discomfort

Once you have identified your triggers and warning signs, and once you have made the commitment to stay present with whatever emotional responses emerge in you, the only thing left to do is follow through with it. Of course, this can seem easier said than done!

This part of the process can feel counterintuitive and, by its very nature, can be emotionally overwhelming. But again, frequent practice along with a willingness to stay with what emerges will eventually help you develop a tolerance for unpleasant emotions.

First, in order to accept an emotion, you need to be able to correctly recognize that it is occurring. Take some time to be still with that sensation, whatever it is. Try not to rush in to deny or avoid it, and remember that there's no need to embrace it either or pretend it isn't there. Simply give yourself and the emotion space to expand and watch. What can you feel in your body? What sort of thoughts are in your mind? How do those thoughts make you feel? Why is this happening to you?

This exercise can be done during a more formal meditation, or you can simply choose to pause and take a moment out of your daily life to gather yourself and become aware of your emotions.

Next, try to gain some distance from the emotion by using imagery. It's so easy to get "swallowed up" by an emotion, feeling as though it is us and that we are completely identified with it. But emotions are temporary and passing. Can you find a way to let the emotion be what it is without getting carried away with it?

For example, our example woman may imagine that all the chatter and chaos and negative emotion of the family holidays is like a dark cloud of tangled words that she can wrap up in a beautiful pink balloon, where, once inside, it goes silent and peaceful. She can then stand outside of these emotions and hold them on a string, apart from herself. Another person might imagine that their sadness and overwhelming depression is really a small, tired person who just wants to sit at the table for a little while. By sitting across from this person and allowing it to speak without getting upset about its existence, we can start to gain some distance and detachment. This is the beginning of emotional mastery.

As you engage with your emotions, whatever they are and in whatever image you have given them, pay close attention to your breath. Being focused on the simple inhale and exhale of your breath can ground you in the moment and remind you to stay anchored in the present. Wait out your emotional spike and see what is on the other side.

Part of the practice of learning to tolerate emotional distress is understanding that it is a practice (i.e. not something you master all at once and never have to look at again). If you are aware and accepting of the fact that you *will* experience emotional comebacks, you can remain calm when they occur and appreciate them for what they are: an opportunity to try again to turn away from avoidance and escape behavior and reaffirm your commitment to yourself.

Emotional strength and the ability to calmly withstand even the most unpleasant emotions is like a muscle: the more you exercise it, the stronger it gets. So be grateful for every opportunity you have to exercise it. If you feel strong emotions arising again, watch yourself closely. Are you frustrated with yourself for not "doing it right"? Are you impatient with the process, feeling like you should have succeeded with it sooner? Great! Take these feelings themselves and feed them back into your practice. Remind yourself of your commitment to doing the opposite of your escape behaviors. Remind yourself that you can and will stay with feelings, and that all feelings, no matter how unpleasant, will pass. Sit with them and observe that past an initial period of high stress and anxiety, they aren't overwhelming experiences— merely uncomfortable.

Step 5: Making Friends with Distress

We are all individuals, and nobody is going to experience distress in quite the same way. The only way to truly understand your own emotional patterns and behaviors is to get in there directly and become aware of them.

These five steps can be thought of as a closed sequence that improves and refines itself every time you go through a cycle. Every time you are able to successfully soothe yourself without avoidance/escape behaviors, take note and remember how you did it. Next time you are in a similar position, you can pull these activities, thoughts, or ideas out of your emotional inventory and use them. In essence, you are building greater awareness of yourself and slowly removing the behavior from the realm of passive, reactionary, and unconscious into the realm of deliberate, conscious action that really serves you.

This final step is about taking stock of what works. This can be actively making a list of behaviors that you want to practice or simply taking a moment to quietly acknowledge progress when it happens. Make a note of words of encouragement, mantras, or images that help you get into the state of mind you're trying to achieve. Write them down somewhere you can easily access, or maybe try carrying a small object that encourages you to stay mindful.

In fact, once you begin to feel more in control, you can start to actively seek out exposure to distress in order to gain practice and strengthen your resilience. Though this may seem scary, in a way, it gives you more control to engineer situations that from the outset have you feeling prepared and confident.

If you'd like to do this, start with your triggers and think of a situation that may make you feel anxious. Of course, it may backfire to throw you in the deep end of distress—instead, think of an ultimate goal that you'd like to achieve and then set up a few gradual steps and smaller goals you can achieve to reach that. This "exposure ladder" is a series of manageable steps that increase in increments. Each step might involve spending more and more time in the distressing situation, or it may entail increasing the intensity of a sensation or an interaction with a triggering person.

As an example, a man might have trouble with watching certain highly charged news shows or movies as a trigger and resort to overeating as an escape behavior. He commits to telling himself that he can, in fact, tolerate the feelings of anxiety and hopelessness this brings up. He sets himself a goal: to be able to watch a full news program without overeating to soothe himself. He starts with smaller steps. First, he watches five minutes. Then he watches two five-minute segments with a break. Then he watches ten uninterrupted minutes. And so on. His goal is not to enjoy the news—just to strengthen his ability to tolerate uncomfortable feelings without succumbing to escape.

Whether you choose to practice an emotional exposure ladder or simply want to do your action plan when distress naturally rears its head, if you can stay with the emotion in the present, breathe, reorient your behavior, and reward any successes, you essentially train yourself toward greater emotional control and stability.

A warning here: this is a technique that's a little more advanced than those in the previous chapters, so it's a good idea to start with those and work your way up. What's important is that you realize you're always the one in control. You want to gently challenge yourself to go out of your comfort zone and push the belief that you can't bear uncertainty—but you don't want to completely overwhelm or terrify yourself, either! Take baby steps, appraise, adjust, and try again. Discomfort, uncertainty, and distress are not your enemies—they are your teachers if you are willing to see them that way.

Detachment and Stoicism

When we speak of the merits of "emotional toughness," the term might be misinterpreted as "coldness and distance" or, worse, "harshness and aggression." There are certainly cases in which efforts to maintain toughness have resulted in actions or statements that are aloof or abusive.

But the kind of resilience we're concerned with isn't something we direct toward others—it's about how we manage ourselves, how we rise to challenges or adversity, and how we persist. It doesn't harm our interpersonal relationships; in fact, it's something that actually improves how we connect and care for ourselves and others.

In this chapter, we'll discuss two similar ways to develop and refine emotional resilience. Both have roots that go back thousands of years, so the fact that we're still talking about them speaks to their lasting influence. One was popularized by the famed philosopher-emperor Marcus Aurelius of ancient Rome, while the other was developed by the one and only Buddha. Both deal with how we perceive the emotional substance of our realities and how regulating our feelings and temper is essential to experiencing a happy life. Additionally, they both work from the perspective of the "vast universe" and our tiny, insignificant place in that universe.

"Attachment is the origin, the root of suffering; hence it is the cause of suffering."
—*The Dalai Lama, 1988*

The tenets of detachment are in the first known volumes of Buddhist thought, the Pāli Canon. It's expressed as *nekkhamma*, which roughly translates to "renunciation." We often refer to this trait as "detachment," but it's perhaps more accurately expressed as "nonattachment."

Nonattachment isn't the same as deprivation. Consider food, for example: we have to eat to preserve ourselves, and there's nothing wrong with enjoying it. What nonattachment *does* address is desire and craving. It's logical to assume that when we cease dependence on certain life conditions, our odds of having a happier existence improve. We may still need it but don't feel emotionally empty without it.

Dependence on External Things

We pin our internal happiness to external people, objects, and circumstances because of the feelings they bring us. We're conditioned to be that way. Getting material goods and emotional satisfaction feeds an internal sense of completion. Once we obtain those things or satisfy those desires, we tend to cling to them for dear life. We fear losing them and stress out over that fear. We feel shattered if we lose something or grieve when a situation changes. Breaking up, getting laid off, and losing a house or a car are major traumatic events.

Our attachment to these feelings defines us. We feel euphoria over positive results and devastation over negative ones. Strangely, we depend on *both* of those feelings, happy and sad, for our own comfort. Wallowing over regrets and disappointments can be a source of safety. The act of suffering can be as cozy and familiar as an easy chair. In trying to hold on to emotional habits, we restrict our ability to experience joy in the present.

When we stop trying to exercise control over the world around us, we actually set ourselves free. We give the world the freedom to fulfill us and remove its power to destroy us. Letting go is letting happiness *in*.

This isn't a quick fix or a one-time decision. It's a commitment that must be deliberately renewed day to day, moment to moment. That in itself is the opposite of instant gratification, which is always temporary. It's something that must be cultivated, not just granted. It's a change to the way you experience and interact with the things and feelings you want.

The Problems with Attachment

Claiming that our unhappiness or depression is caused by attachment may still seem contradictory. Isn't getting what we want a good thing? Doesn't it drive us to work harder to achieve a physical level of comfort? Doesn't it reinforce our values?

Attachment plays a role in the conflicts over daily issues and occasional events. For example, arguments with others arise from our strict attachment to our opinions. When something doesn't go our way, we get angry because of our attachment to the results we want. When we lose something we cherish, we feel sad because we're no longer attached to those objects. Our agony over losing a loved one comes from their attachment to our lives.

This isn't a criticism of the emotions we feel toward people or things. Love, enjoyment, intelligence, and comfort are not disorders or adverse conditions. Rather, we're discussing the reliance itself—the fact that our peace of mind *depends* on fulfilling those needs and our fixation on doing so.

Attachment to People

We may bristle at the suggestion that our attachment to *people* is an issue, but it's just as problematic. In fact, it could be *more* dangerous because humans are more unpredictable and susceptible to change. We're driven by nature, and nature changes all the time.

Attachment to others is a bred condition, not something that occurs overnight. We develop feelings by spending time with someone. With partners, we gain affection; with coworkers, we build cooperation; with friends and family, we gain enjoyment and sentiment.

But in all those situations, we're not really attaching to the people—we're attaching to the *experience.* Our connection is with the emotions we feel when we're with them, good or bad. Our mind identifies pleasant sensations, so we crave them more often. But as those attachments grow and deepen, we start to nurture discomfort and fear losing those pleasures. We believe our happiness rests with their presence, and that leads us to think we need an outside factor to be contented. By doing so, we forfeit our own power to make ourselves happy.

Connection versus Entanglement

Attachment puts us in a state of need. Everything we do and think is focused on the thing we're attached to. Our perspective blurs, and our connections with others turn into entanglements.

When we experience connection, we share bonds and commonalities but maintain our individuality. Our overattachment to the feelings we experience can distort that connection into codependency. We start thinking in terms of demands or needs. That's when we stop feeling connected and begin feeling *entangled*.

This is when we perceive external forces as things we need to be happy. But nothing outside of us can truly bring happiness or security. The only ones in control of our own happiness are ourselves—our dependence on others might obscure that fact, but it doesn't change it.

As our attachments grow, our expectations become more fixed in our minds. Our fear of losing what we desire becomes more acute. We become concerned that the person or thing we're attached to may fall short of our needs, if it is not lost altogether. The experience can be painful.

When that worry manifests, our mind puts us in "survival mode." We become focused, obsessed, and maybe even addicted to the objects of our attachment. We become clingy, controlling, domineering, and insecure. Such emotions lead to near-dysfunction and disrupt our balance, and we act irrationally.

Pain and Suffering is a Choice

We choose to experience misery and hurt. Believe it or not, that's good news. We can avoid entanglement by living with nonattachment. That doesn't mean we withdraw or isolate ourselves from others and never connect with anyone again. It doesn't mean we sacrifice our dreams or aspirations. It doesn't mean we devalue love, support, association, or compassion.

What it *does* mean is that we release our *need* for the relationship or thing that we've become attached to. We accept things as they are and recognize that the situations in our existence will constantly evolve and change. Permanence is illusory—everything is temporary.

Accepting this viewpoint isn't automatic or easy. It requires letting go of details we feel strongly about but can't control. It's tough because our egos are constantly fed by the drive to *keep* that control. Releasing that need and putting our trust in the universe is a tough task. But the reality is that we really have no choice in what happens in our lives. We can either fight it or embrace it. When we detach, we embrace anything that comes, and we make the choice to find happiness in any situation.

Breaking Attachment

Detachment can be frightening, but it's much easier than it sounds. We don't just disengage with people or things—we merely change how we relate to them. Nobody feels *glad* about being dependent. Even if we claim to be happy, circumstances or events will arise that will expose that happiness as a fraud. Dependence only feels good when everything's going in our favor. When conditions change, or when people leave, that dependence becomes a source of anxiety.

Detachment relieves us of our expectations. Our happiness isn't based on need; it becomes authentic. We don't rely on things outside us to make us happy because we're complete as we are. We can achieve happiness on our own. Happiness from outside factors becomes an *addition* to our positive state of mind, not the only source for it. The following steps can help you develop a healthy detachment that will inform and reinforce your life and relationships.

Awareness. Look at the attachments you have in your life—your partner, your surroundings, your social circles, or your work. Where have you given up power? Do you expect something from those relationships or things? Is any part of your connection controlled by your fear, anxiety, or insecurity? Find out which situations you might need to detach from.

Examination. Now that you've identified these attachments, inspect them more closely. What fuels your attachment? Do fear or insecurity play a part? How valid are your fears? If you sense they're irrational, then what are you *really* worried about? Take a lot of time with this step.

Acceptance. Accept each moment exactly for what it is. Don't compare or try to turn it into yesterday—that's gone. Don't try to extend the moment into something that will last forever, because it won't. Absorb the moment fully and enjoy it because it will pass.

Now is enough. Tomorrow will never be the same as today. Relationships will end;

others will begin. Your surroundings will change. You'll be able to deal with those changes when they come. But right now, in the present moment, appreciate and enjoy what you have. No matter what the future holds, what you have now will always be enough.

Practice letting things be. Make peace with the moment. Don't worry if something's wrong with you or your life. Operate from a standpoint of acceptance. This doesn't mean you can't work toward creating a better tomorrow or improving yourself. It just means accepting where you are now as the foundation for your achievements.

Release the need to know. Life will always be uncertain. Obsessing about tomorrow is self-defeating; there will always be another tomorrow after it. You can make projections and predictions about the future, and you might be right. But you can't affect them until they happen. The best way to be prepared is to work on what's before you right now.

If conventional Buddhist thoughts on detaching can be briefly summed up, it's about recognizing that everything good and bad in this world fades as quickly as it comes. We have no choice or control in it either way. Thus, we cannot expect what we want to happen, no matter how reasonable it is. The moment we form an expectation, we form an attachment to an outcome, and that makes you vulnerable to suffering (and emotionality). You can struggle and still receive a negative outcome, or you can embrace it as it comes.

The Value of Neutrality

Buddhist detachment can be difficult to wrap your mind around, but the essential idea is very similar to that of Stoicism. Stoicism is a way of viewing life and seeing your place in the world, and it was originally put into words by the Athenian philosopher Zeno around the third century BCE.

Stoic philosophy argues that unchecked emotions are some of the biggest enemies of your happiness and fulfillment.

Rationality, perspective, and practicality are what drive Stoicism.

According to Stoicism, you have the utmost free will in any circumstance, regardless of what your emotions might tell you. There is your *emotional* reality and the *objective* reality, and you can choose which you want to abide by. You have more control of what's going on in your life than you realize. Actually, you can choose the emotions you feel.

There are many ways to characterize Stoicism, but I find it best to break it into two primary tenets.

The first important tenet of Stoicism that will seek to promote emotional resilience is that everything that happens in the world is neutral—every event and consequence thereof. Every event has a different effect on everyone, but the events themselves are neutral, without intent, and play no favorites. There is no bad or good; it is all subjective. It is created with you, along with all emotions and judgments.

This means that it's your reaction and perception that cause your unhappiness. If you perceive events to be negative, they will be negative. If you perceive them to be positive, you will find the positive in them.

If you are sitting in a café and a car slams into your parked car on the street outside, you have a choice about how you will respond. It's a neutral event, and you can attach any set of emotions to it you want.

You can react the way most people do and freak out or play the victim, or you can calmly take out your phone and solve the problem by researching new cars with upgraded sound systems. The operative facts are the same, yet two very different outcomes will ensue. Which reaction do you think will lead to a more orderly resolution of what just happened?

No matter how you react, the facts will remain the same: your car is going to need repairs or will need to be replaced.

Your emotional stability hinges upon your reaction and perception of neutral events, and every event is neutral. It's your response and opinion about the event that either causes you tremendous emotional distress or leads you to a quick resolution with minimal stress. Taking ownership of your role in your level of happiness and stability is why the same event can affect people in drastically different ways.

What makes things negative, unpleasant, and stressful is our judgment of those otherwise neutral events. We don't have control over most of the situations we are put into, despite our best efforts. You can't control other people or the weather—if you feel that you do, you are fighting a losing battle because you are setting yourself up for continual disappointment. But we do have control over one hundred percent of our reactions and responses to those situations. This is a process that can make or break your mood and perception of life.

People react in predictable ways when things they perceive to be negative happen. They either blame someone else, or they beat themselves up emotionally. Because of that lack of control over events, many are frustrated by their feelings of helplessness. Focus instead on how you respond to what's taking place right now in your life.

Outside forces are not out to make you miserable. Even if they are, you are making the choice to feel that emotion. Look within. The world hands us a blank slate every morning; you are the sole writer and editor of what is written on that slate. Some people will inevitably see the silver lining of a storm cloud, while others are overwhelmed by the smallest hint of darkness. Which will you be?

"If you are pained by any external thing, it is not this thing that disturbs you, but your own judgment about it. And it is in your power to wipe out this judgment now."
– Marcus Aurelius

The second tenet of Stoicism is to always temper your expectations and expect difficulty and challenge. This isn't necessarily about being pessimistic; it's more about being realistic and steeling yourself for the hardships you'll encounter. It's amazing what adjusted expectations can do for your outlook: how would you feel if you won the lottery and expected to win versus if you won the lottery and forgot you had even bought a ticket?

Many of us are waking up with the former expectation—that life will or should deliver us something. It's a dangerous place to be. When you can move away from this thinking and ask yourself, "What's the worst that can happen?" you'll be prepared and unsurprised. Imagine yourself suffering, think about your death, and even practice a degree of abstinence or deprivation in your life. How will you feel afterward? As you may have surmised, Stoicism is a particularly helpful tool in battling the obstacles we face in our lives.

Going a step further, you can, as the Stoics say, *turn the obstacle upside down*. Train yourself to avoid judging events as purely good or bad. In fact, realize you can even turn all obstacles upside down, looked at through another perspective, to suit your purposes. This means that anything that seems to present an obstacle should actually be seen as an opportunity for something positive and growth oriented. Remember, it is your interpretation of entirely neutral events.

So look at what happens objectively and dispassionately—it might be raining. And then choose your best reaction. The world won't end, and the activities you had planned for outdoors can be done another day. How might the rain force you to get creative or explore other untapped potential? What are the alternate perspectives you can adopt, rather than one of sadness or frustration? These alternate perspectives always exist, and you should train your ability to see them.

The truth is that you always have the ability to respond in a way that amounts to rolling with the punches. How might this obstacle become an opportunity, if only an opportunity to practice your sense of resilience and patience?

The most practical effect is enabling the sufferer (so to speak) to become immune to negative emotional spirals. Instead, they force themselves to engage in alternative thought patterns to gain perspective and move forward rationally. For example, imagine you are a nurse and you have a patient who is very cranky. The reason you approached this person is because you wanted to help them. But this person is being surly, doesn't want to cooperate, or even tries to bully you. In short, this person is being mean and nasty.

According to the Stoics, instead of feeling hassled or feeling that this person is making your life difficult, try to think of this person as actually helping you out. How can that be? Well, this person's behavior is giving you a tremendous opportunity to exercise new virtues that you should have more of in your life, like being understanding, patient, and compassionate.

Another example drawn from Stoic teachings is the death of a loved one. If you love somebody, it's easy to fall into despair when they pass away. But you could use this loss as an opportunity to show fortitude. Instead of feeling pain and loss, you can look at this commonly negative situation as an opportunity to practice inner strength, calm, control, equanimity, and level-headedness.

Our life is full of teachable moments, like the parables of old or Aesop's Fables. Regardless of how negative a particular event may seem, you can always try to reinterpret it as a positive opportunity or look at the other side of the situation. The more you turn the obstacle upside down, the more you'll realize that there really is no such thing as good and bad. It all depends on how you choose to perceive something.

For centuries, Stoicism has been a virtual antidote for emotional disruptions that can plague any of us. It tells you that you unequivocally have the power to create your own reality. Meanwhile, Buddhist principles also make it clear that your surroundings don't need to change for change to occur. Your mental state is freer than you think, and sometimes a mental switch is all it takes for resilience to spring forth.

Be Grateful and Savor Life

Remember your brain's hardwired fascination with bad news? Gratitude and acceptance might not look like they have much to do with combatting anxiety, but the mindset that accompanies gratitude can be thought of as a direct antidote to this negativity bias, because it forces us to dwell on and appreciate good things we usually ignore in favor of focusing on the bad.

We associate the emotion of gratitude with thankfulness for whatever comes into our lives, positive or not. Although the adage of being grateful for what we have is well known, it's not always a practice we grasp, even though there's *always* something to be grateful for. Still, studies have shown that just being aware of or questioning your gratitude—even if you can't think of anything off the top of your head—can create some powerful chemical changes.

For example, stop reading for a minute and consider five things you're grateful for. They don't need to be big accomplishments or achievements; they can be simple parts of everyday living. "I have clean air to breathe," "I have family and friends who love me," "I have a place to sleep," "I live in interesting times."

Now compare this to the everyday life of someone in abject poverty who's struggling to make ends meet and is on the brink of starvation. Or consider the tale of a ballet dancer who had to have her feet amputated (or something similarly morbid and unfortunate).

You might not have noticed any immediate changes, but a feeling of acceptance and perspective probably just entered your mind. You may not have everything that you want (none of us ever do), but your life is still pretty darn good. Yes, even factoring in all those other things you worry about!

And it's been scientifically proven that gratitude is more or less a natural antidepressant. Thinking about or asking what you're grateful for actually activates certain neural circuits that produce dopamine and serotonin, the neurotransmitters that regulate our pleasure centers and mood levels. They then travel the neural pathways to the "bliss" center of the brain, much like a prescribed antidepressant. The more you stimulate them, the stronger and more automatic they become, and the more your resilience and calm become a natural way of living.

Hebb's law states, "Neurons that fire together wire together." We see this proverb at work in everyday life. When you're walking through a forest for the first time, you're forging a new path that can provide challenges. But the more the path is traveled, the more defined and easier to follow it becomes.

So it works with the human brain. The more a neural pathway is activated, the less effort it takes to animate it the next time. Since the practice of mental gratitude greases the neurons, simple, short daily meditations on your appreciation can actually ease your tension on a biological level.

Dopamine in particular is extraordinarily useful in attitude enhancement. It's called the "reward" neurotransmitter because it feels good to get. But it also helps initiate action, and increasing it makes you more likely to do whatever made you happier. It's like the brain saying, "That thing you just did? Yeah, do that again!"

The downside is that negative thought patterns activate *their* neural pathways as well. When we constantly see the negative aspects of a situation and seek out problems, the neural paths for negative thinking grow stronger. Proactively applying gratitude can train our brains to seek out constructive elements in our lives while lessening the destructive ones. We water the flowers instead of watering the weeds.

Researchers Robert A. Emmons and Michael E. McCullough performed a study in 2003 called "Counting Blessings Versus Burdens: An Experimental Investigation of Gratitude and Subjective Well-Being in Daily Life." They gathered a group of young adults and told them to keep journals. One group was instructed to write daily entries of things they were grateful for, and the other was told to write about their annoyances or why they were better off than other people.

The researchers' instructions to the gratitude journalists encouraged them to note any facet of their lives that they were grateful for, regardless of importance: "There are many things in our lives, both large and small, that we might be grateful about. Think back over the past week and write down on the lines below up to five things in your life that you are grateful or thankful for."

For journalists who were given the task of writing down their annoyances, the researchers said, "Hassles are irritants— things that annoy or bother you. They occur in various domains of life, including relationships, work, school, housing, finances, health, and so forth. Think back over today and, on the lines below, list up to five hassles that occurred in your life." The results were predictably persuasive. The gratitude journalists showed greater increases in determination, attention, enthusiasm, and energy. Their findings showed gratitude to be a powerful social and spiritual accelerator:

The experience of gratitude, and the actions stimulated by it, build and strengthen social bonds and friendships. Moreover, encouraging people to focus on the benefits they have received from others leads them to feel loved and cared for by others . . . Therefore, gratitude appears to build friendships and other social bonds. These are social resources because, in times of need, these social bonds are wellsprings to be tapped for the provision of social support. Gratitude, thus, is a form of love, a consequence of an already formed attachment as well as a precipitating condition for the formation of new affectional bonds . . . Gratitude is also likely to build and strengthen a sense of spirituality, given the strong historical association between gratitude and religion . . . Finally, to the extent that gratitude, like other positive emotions, broadens the scope of cognition and enables flexible and creative thinking, it also facilitates coping with stress and adversity.

Just as tellingly, the study proved that realizing that other people were worse off does *not* equal gratitude. Rather, gratitude is an appreciation of the positive aspects of your own situation.

Emmons and McCullough's findings could inspire you to try journaling yourself. Putting your thoughts in writing is almost always a good practice.

Start out by replicating the exercise at the beginning of this chapter: write down five things that you're grateful for. Make a conscious effort to reflect upon the things that bring you joy, elation, or peace of mind. As we've said, there's *always* something to be thankful for in a given situation. It might bring you additional perspective to write five things you have that most people do *not* have. Sometimes it's only through contrast that we can truly keep gratitude in mind.

Commit to this practice every day for the next ten days. Keep a journal by your bed and take a minute before sleeping to recall the events of the day that made you smile.

Or start a list on your smartphone to write pleasant events down as they happen (also a nice way for a quick pick-me-up when you're not having a great day). You can also find an "accountability partner" to keep a list like yours. Every week, you can check in for five minutes and read your lists to each other.

This practice can turn gratitude into your own mental gym—strength training for your neural pathways. The more you practice the act of gratitude, the healthier that muscle gets. Just like in physical gyms, the more you show up and work the gratitude angle, the easier the workouts get. And the less power your negativity and anxiety bias has over you.

If writing feels like too much, you can ease into gratitude practice with an extremely uncomplicated daily exercise: every time your feet hit the ground after you get out of bed, simply say thank you. Nature likes to be appreciated and paid attention to in the same way that humans do. Acknowledging nature helps our own lives bloom in response.

We get used to whatever situations surround us without much effort. Initiating gratitude in all walks of our own lives might be a more trying task or even impractical in certain situations. When was the last time you turned the key in your car's ignition and praised the miracles of the internal combustion engine? Have you ever taken a walk through a city park and expressed thanks for arch supports? Do you take time from work to appreciate the craft and convenience of your hole punch or stapler?

But in truth, those are all perfectly fine things to be grateful for—especially when we don't have them. Natural disasters like hurricanes or earthquakes can give affected people a new appreciation for things like running water and electricity. It's true that nothing should be taken for granted—but realistically, that feeling doesn't necessarily last for long. A few days removed from those disasters, you're back to cursing the elevator if it takes more than thirty seconds to get to your floor.

The central point is that gratitude is easy to execute but not always easy to maintain. There's nothing wrong with expressing annoyances over little inconveniences, but letting those irritations inform the core of our beings is ill-advised. Letting them morph into great anxiety-inducing monsters not only feels bad, but also prevents us from giving the respect and gratitude we should to all those things that are actually going well for us. We've seen how our brain transforms itself based on even our smallest impulses. If we can make gratitude a more constant and consistent impulse, our brains will see to it that our happiness improves.

Studies have also been conducted to understand the benefits of *savoring*—the mental and emotional act of appreciating a particular experience while you are currently engaging in it. It can be said to be gratitude in real time.

One such study investigated a group of depressed participants who were asked to take their time and relish an activity they normally hurry to get through. The activities were all part of their daily functions: eating a meal, taking a shower, finishing a work assignment, or walking to a subway or bus stop. The subjects were told to write down how they felt after extending these routines and how those feelings compared to those when they rushed through them.

Another study surveyed members of a community who were comparatively healthy in their states of mind. These participants were told to savor two pleasant experiences each day simply by reflecting on them for two to three minutes and trying to make the pleasure last as long and intensely as possible.

The results for both studies were dramatic: taking time to savor certain events, even ones normally associated with routine and tasks, increased the participants' overall happiness and decreased their depression to some extent. The simple act of slowing down and being intentional with their actions improved how they felt about, well, everything.

The Journal of Positive Psychology noted that these and other findings supported the theory that "savoring responses is an important mechanism by which individuals transmute the raw stuff of daily life into positive effect." In other words, savoring in itself is a pleasurable activity. Savoring is a way to add and reinforce another layer of emotional benefit to an act of pleasure on top of the sensual and mental enjoyment that such acts provide.

Taking time to finish and appreciate a meal or dessert is an obvious example of physical savoring, but it's not the only one. Focusing, even meditating, on the character and nature of things we do and see ramps up the benefits as well. Viewing human drama from a park bench, experiencing the rush of breeze and motion in a bike ride, noting the give and take in a group conversation with friends—all are activities that can be transformed by stretching them out and appreciating each part. In reality, savoring is the act of stepping outside of your brain and anxieties and putting your focus onto a single pleasurable thing.

Reflecting and communicating our appreciation of these experiences is another way to savor them after the fact. Whether one writes their thoughts down in a blog, talks about their experience to friends, or merely meditates and gives thanks privately, they add another, deeper level to the episodes that make up their lives. The act of savoring can lead to a more conscious state of mind in which we have clearer, sharper interactions with the world and find more to appreciate about it. You'll be more self-aware, and that means more able to step in and stop the anxiety spiral before it even starts.

Three-Step Cognitive Behavioral Therapy

CBT is evidence-based and well-suited to tackling the inner dialogue that accompanies worry, anxiety, regret, shame, grief, guilt, blame, and low self-esteem. Life is filled with challenges, adversities, and unexpected events. These can either be viewed as painful and unfair, or manageable and growth-inspiring—all depending on the mindset we cultivate with our self-talk.

When it comes to anxiety, CBT can help by inviting you to slow down and rewrite some of the programming behind anxious rumination and panic.

CBT is not about "thinking positively" but thinking more clearly, realistically, and neutrally—without cognitive distortions. In CBT, our thoughts, feelings, and behavior are all interconnected, i.e. if we can change our thoughts, we can change our feelings and consequently how we act (and vice versa).

You may already be familiar with certain cognitive distortions—catastrophizing, black-and-white thinking, etc.—and have begun recognizing the language of negative self-talk in yourself. Observing your thinking and becoming aware of previously automatic thoughts and distortions is step 1.

Step 2 is learning to gently and consistently challenge these thoughts and their underlying core beliefs, testing just how accurate they are. We considered this in the previous chapter where we asked ourselves questions, tested our assumptions, and encouraged ourselves to seek alternatives.

Step 3 is doing the work of replacing these distorted thoughts and beliefs with ones that are healthier, more accurate, and more likely to lead to a balanced and optimistic life. Before we move on to this very important step, however, we need to look a little closer at the language of negative self-talk, and how to spot triggers and warning signs so that we can step in and stop cognitive distortions *before* they take flight in our minds.

If your anxious rumination takes the form of negative and pessimistic self-talk, the following may be very helpful.

Step 1: Observe

Self-talk is made of words. That's all it is.

It's literally like a film script that you run internally. But words can be edited, deleted, rewritten. In previous sections, we've focused on fact versus fiction and the importance of comparing our thoughts against objective reality as much as possible. This is a way of fine-tuning the *content* of our thoughts, but there's also the question of the style, grammar, vocabulary, and tone of the language we use when we talk to ourselves.

You've utterly failed, you big fat idiot.

You didn't pass the quiz that time.

Both of these statements can refer to the same event and, in a way, are factually equivalent—i.e. "didn't pass" is the same as "failed." However, it's obvious that they carry very different emotional nuances and will have very different effects on the person thinking them.

Automatic negative self-talk has a certain flavor that you can recognize with practice. It's usually short, spontaneous, and emotionally loaded with strong words, or has a rambling, looping quality. It's filled with overgeneralizing language like *always, never, nobody, should, nothing, must, completely*, or language filled with guilt, self-flagellation, and judgment.

Watch for language that spirals or feeds on itself or steadily mounts in intensity. Look out for thoughts that you accept as true immediately in the moment without a second thought. Automatic thoughts are usually strongly infused with feelings of fear, anger or shame, and will appear in language that suggests this—at the very least, you'll know it's negative self-talk simply because you feel awful when you listen to it!

Step 2: Challenge

If you catch yourself in negative self-talk—congratulations. Even better, however, would be to avoid it altogether, or stop it before it happens using your knowledge of what usually triggers these thoughts for you. Negative thoughts are easier to recognize and handle when they are still small.

As a technique, "thought stopping" appeared in the late 1950s in the sport psychology world and was used to cut short self-defeating and anxious thoughts that got in the way of performance. An excellent overview can be found in Zinsser, Bunker, and Williams' 2010 book, *Cognitive*

Techniques for Building Confidence and Enhancing Performance. The idea is to use a behavioral or mental cue to snap out of a negative self-talk spiral.

For those suffering from mental health issues like panic disorders, it can be especially hard to distract yourself once a negative thought appears in your mind. This technique acts as a tool to help become aware of and then replace these thoughts in a way similar to practicing mindfulness.

Pinching yourself, imagining a red light, or saying "stop" out loud can all act as cues to bring your conscious awareness to the moment and away from negative self-talk.

It's essentially the art of beneficial distraction, and even more effective when you then quickly redirect your attention to a preferable subject (a more realistic thought, perhaps?). It's an assertive stance you are taking against that inner dialogue that you know only carries you to places you don't want to go.

The technique can potentially backfire if you end up constantly monitoring yourself to look for failures you can pounce on—the trick is to bring mindfulness to the process, not punishment or judgment. If you try this technique for a while and find it actually worsens the problem, ease up, be more compassionate, or simply attempt a different technique. Thought stopping may help for more superficial rumination, but not for deeper anxieties that may respond better to slow, deliberate engagement.

If you'd like to try the technique, however, here's how to begin:

Write down a list of all the most distressing, recurring, distracting, and unwanted thoughts you wish to stop paying attention to. Try to rank them from most to least distressing. Include anything from: "One day, my boss is going to figure out how inept I am and fire me," to, "This lump probably means cancer."

Next, do some prep work by practicing—sit alone in a private room and spend some time visualizing any situation in life where the most distressing thought might conceivably intrude. For a while, go into the thought and focus on it, feeling out its contours. Then, as abruptly as you can, stop the thought.

Stand up quickly, say, "Stop!" out loud, snap your eyes open, make a loud clapping noise, or click your fingers. Empty your mind and try to hold that emptiness for thirty seconds or so. If the thought tries to intrude again, repeat "stop" as often as necessary.

What you are trying to do is gain practice at stopping rumination mid-thought. In time, you can be less drastic with your interruption, and eventually internalize the "stop" so you only say it quietly to yourself. You don't necessarily need to use the word *stop*—you could also visualize your thoughts as traffic that stops dutifully at a red light. Try saying out loud, "I'm having a thought about XYZ right now," to remind yourself that it's just a thought, and to gain distance.

Whatever you do, simply remind yourself that thoughts are just words—just a script that you can stop in its tracks and rewrite. The hard work is to recognize the thought, but once you do, realize it has no hold on you unless you pay attention to it. Make a habit of using certain phrases to interrupt unwanted thoughts, divert your attention, and affirm your *choice* to follow certain thoughts and drop others:

Don't go there

Let it be

Let it go

It's in the past

Leave it alone

Focus

Don't pay attention

Slow down

This, too, will pass

It doesn't matter

Breathe

You've got this

Using this thought-stopping technique may make some people uncomfortable—aren't you just ignoring your problems?

It's worth remembering that thought stopping is best used for those thoughts that you know are intrusive, unwanted, and genuinely unhelpful. These are the thoughts that you have already identified as irrational, untrue, or exaggerated, and you know that entertaining them will only lead to stress and worry.

Your goal is to tolerate and manage anxiety, rather than turn a blind eye to it. Similarly, having thought stopping in your mental toolkit doesn't mean you are unable to hear your own intuition or engage when a situation warrants genuine concern. Thought stopping is merely a mental fuse that lets you halt catastrophic rumination before you get too carried away with it.

For some people, the thought-stopping technique outlined above may feel a little punitive and may not work for them. Thankfully, there are plenty of other techniques underpinned by the same principles. You could try scattered counting, for example. Counting to ten is a common anger management technique, but it's easy enough to become automatic, allowing your brain to carry on ruminating even as you count. Rather, jump around with random numbers to engage your thoughts more, e.g. "43, 12, 5, 88, 356, 90, 5 . . ."

In the same way, a mantra or spoken word can interrupt runaway thoughts—choose a more complicated nonsense phrase or something in another language to prevent yourself from doing it too automatically. Alternatively, you can select affirmations based on your specific triggers or perceived negative qualities. Though they can take time to work, the reason so many find them effective is that our brains eventually come to think of them as true. These affirmations can be specific quotes from religious texts, or statements like: "I believe in myself," and, "I am in charge of my thoughts." These can be recited both mentally and out loud, but with conviction. Repeating lines you don't really believe will be pointless, so choose your affirmations wisely.

You could try self-soothing with encouraging positive self-talk, such as: "Don't worry, you can handle this," or, "You're doing great!" Play a song you like or listen to a podcast to engage your auditory channels and pull attention away from anxious overthinking.

A distracting cue can also be physical in nature—physically move yourself into a different position, get up and do a few jumping jacks, or go for a quick jog outside to break out of thought loops. You can also switch to more bodily/somatic awareness by simply focusing on your breath and practicing a technique called muscle isolation.

Sit or lie comfortably, close your eyes, and then work your way through all your muscles, starting from the ones in your toes. Squeeze them as tightly as you can for five seconds and then release and relax completely. Then focus on the muscles in your feet and legs, moving up until you reach the muscles in your face and scalp. Not only will this help immensely to release physical tension, but it will distract your overactive mind and bring it more fully into the present moment.

Muscle isolation can be an excellent warmup to a more formal sitting meditation practice, or a great way to end a mindfulness session. Combine it with gentle soothing music or head outside where you can feel the sun and breeze on your skin.

Another classic CBT technique is to decide that instead of stopping or running away from scary and overwhelming thoughts, you'll simply stare them down and ask what's the worst that could happen. Look squarely at your ruminations and say, *so what?* It's rarely as bad as you think, and seldom something you truly cannot handle. Research has found that even those who lose their limbs or eyesight—suffering tragedies anyone would consider horrifying—soon return to a median level of happiness because of how powerful our modes of adaptation are. As such, no matter what it is you're worried over, you're very likely to be able to survive it just fine even if the event were to occur.

You might like to visualize yourself actually encountering the worst-case scenario with grace and poise, tackling the problem and seeing that it isn't in fact the end of the world, even if the worst does come to pass. This alone can take the steam out of your most catastrophic ruminations.

Step 3: Replace

Some thoughts are so useless and untrue that they can be discarded immediately, or stopped using any of the techniques described above. With practice, you'll be able to recognize totally harmful thoughts (like, "I'm probably going to die," or, "Everyone hates me") and release them immediately.

Some ideas and thoughts, however, are a little more subtle and are more appropriately rewritten rather than discarded entirely. These thoughts are often those that we believe have a grain of truth to them. Here, it's necessary to practice a degree of conscious discernment to determine what kind of life script will serve you best. Again, this is a step that can only be done *after* you've gained a good awareness of the kinds of self-talk you engage in—otherwise, you risk having these techniques exacerbate rather than solve the problem.

Exercise 1: Think it through

This exercise takes some time and effort. The first step is to note down your self-talk using any of the methods already discussed (for example, by using a bullet journal, writing down your core beliefs, or periodically taking a self-esteem inventory). Then, after a week, try to look for particular themes or patterns.

What kind of self-talk is it (for example, catastrophizing or mindreading)?

What events, thoughts, feelings, people, or situations triggered the self-talk?

What common threads can you identify?

What was the effect or result of these thoughts?

What do they say about your core beliefs?

Reflect on what you see. Get some distance on your thoughts. This way, we're more likely to evaluate them truthfully, as opposed to in the moment when our feelings might cloud our judgement. Notice if your self-talk has actually held you back in life or made you feel bad. Ask yourself, how would it feel to have positive self-talk instead? What might your life look like and what could you achieve if you didn't limit yourself in this way?

In thinking through things carefully, the more positive alternative is likely to appear to you. For example, you may see that you constantly exaggerate physical symptoms and then get stuck in doom-and-gloom thought loops about what might happen if you fall ill. Seeing all this objectively noted on paper, seeing how it negatively impacts your life in many ways, and seeing how utterly irrational it is, you slowly begin to loosen the self-talk's hold on you.

By completing this exercise, you can begin to see the more accurate and realistic options available to you. Better yet, when you try them out and monitor yourself for a week, you may be surprised to learn just how much wasted mental energy and anguish you can avoid by consciously and deliberately dropping negative self-talk.

Attention Training

One final approach we'll consider here is something we've already talked about with worry postponement, and that is the ability to "train" one's attention. The funny thing about the mind is that it can unhinge itself from the brain in a way. Though your body is (and always is) embedded in the present moment, your mind can detach and float off somewhere else. It can flit to the past and worry about things that have happened, or run ahead to a possible future and stress about that. Or it can float around vaguely in hypotheticals and possibilities that don't strictly belong anywhere.

We are reminded again of the image of the mind being a poorly trained dog on a leash: it goes *everywhere*! Actually, the one place the dog can't seem to be able to go is calmly

144

by your side. Any new smell, any squirrel that dashes across the path, any other passing dog—all capture focus, distract, and divert attention. With an anxious brain, the one place it can't seem to be is calmly in the present.

Just as you need to consistently train a dog to heel, you need to consistently train your attention to focus on what you want it to focus on.

In the chapter that follows, we'll look closely at more formal styles of meditation, but we can use more informal mindfulness practices every day and in every activity. Let's talk about what's called "mundane task focusing." Here, we bed down our attention into the present moment and whatever sensations are occurring there, with acceptance and without judgment, avoidance, or interpretation. When you are mindful, you are also aware of every time your mind runs after a squirrel, so to speak, and can gently bring yourself back to the present.

Think of a mundane task, such as getting dressed, washing dishes, brushing your teeth, or waiting at a traffic light. You're used to doing these things on autopilot. Usually, the mind wanders and, before you know it, finds itself snared in an anxiety spiral. That's why you can also think of these moments as a chance to exercise your attention muscle. Try the following:

First, note down one or two mundane tasks you'd like to work with; for example, taking the dog for a walk. At first, merely notice. See where you are by appraising how much of your attention is going to the task in front of you and how much to mental chatter based in the past or future, in terms of a percentage. Don't do anything yet, just notice.

Next time you perform this mundane task, though, do your attentional workout. When you notice attention wandering, bring it back. How? Well, there is always one sure-fire way to get back into the present. Remember that your mind can wander, but *your body is always in the present*. And your body connects to the present via its five senses. Tune in to your senses, and you are instantly back in the present again.

If your mind wanders, chose any sense and dwell on it:

Touch – feel the texture of the dog leash in your hand or the breeze against your face.

Sight – notice the shade of green of the light on the leaves or the pattern the grass makes on the horizon.

Sound – hear the distant rumble of traffic or the hum of tiny bugs.

Smell – notice that, even though it doesn't seem like it at first, the plain air itself seems to have a smell. Notice it entering and leaving your nostrils.

Taste – you're not eating anything, but notice the lingering sensations on your tongue. Can you still taste the coffee you sipped twenty minutes earlier?

Zoom in on these sensations and simply be aware. We'll explore "sensory anchoring" in a later chapter, but for now, it's enough to simply notice. You don't have to pass judgment either way on what you perceive, or try to interpret it or act on it. Watch the sensation arise but then let it go when it does. You might also like to turn *inward* with your awareness—what physical sensations can you detect in your gut, behind your eyes, in the weight and feeling of your body in space and how it moves? We talk about five senses, but there are in fact many more—can you notice the blurring of senses as they come together to create your total experience of the moment?

Practice this a few times and then conduct another appraisal. What percentage of your attention went to the task at hand versus to unconscious distractions? What have you learned from your mini workouts in the realm of the "mundane"?

It's not strictly necessary, but you might like to keep a diary to record your observations with your attentional training. Note the date and time, the mundane task with which you practiced your training, the duration you sustained, and any comments. You might like to note the kinds of thoughts that continually vied for your attention, and how successful you were at pulling your focus away from them. You might note what worked and didn't, and also the emotions you felt before and after the task. How does focusing on the present feel emotionally? How does your body respond? Even better, do you notice that these discrete exercises change the way your attention is behaving in other areas of life, and with other mundane tasks?

Summary

- Uncertainty, discomfort, and negative emotions are a part of life, and sometimes anxiety is unavoidable, but we can "debug the machine" that is our brain and choose to adopt a mindset that works for us.
- Distress tolerance means accepting that distress is part of life, but also knowing that we can endure it and thrive regardless. We can identify triggers and warning signs, and then deliberately choose not to escape into overthinking, avoidance, or self-soothing behaviors, but sit with our distress. By accepting our feelings, we minimize the power anxiety has over us, and teach ourselves that we are competent to withstand what life throws our way.

- Detachment comes from Buddhist theory or the writing of the ancient Stoics. In their respective ways, they teach us to build inner resilience. Pain is inevitable, but in attaching to it, we cause suffering, which is a choice. We can decide to cultivate emotional serenity and equanimity. With conscious awareness, we can break our attachment and simply accept reality for what it is.
- Neutrality is the commitment to facing life as it is, and realizing that events are neutral, and it is our mental and emotional interpretation that decides whether they are good or bad. Outside forces do not make us anxious, rather our own thoughts and beliefs do, and we have control over those. Realizing this, we understand that we have the power to create our reality.
- Gratitude and the ability to savor life pulls us out of anxious rumination and overthinking and counteracts our natural bias for the negative. By dwelling on the good things in life, we remind ourselves of our blessings, foster positive emotions, and counteract negativity.

- We can use CBT to unpick the negative and unhelpful thoughts and feelings we have about reality with neutrality and awareness. We can observe our thoughts, challenge them (they are not the same as reality!), and then replace them with something deliberately more adaptive and realistic.
- We can **train** our attention, rather than letting it run wild, dragging our wellbeing with it. We can do this by focusing our five senses on a mundane task and bringing our awareness back to the simple present.

Chapter 4. Mindfulness Meditation for Overthinking and Stress

When we talk about the training of attention, the deliberate practice of postponing worries, the observation of inner reactions rather than identifying with and attaching to them, and the commitment to becoming aware of the anxiety loops we get caught in, we are in essence talking about mindfulness.

It's an oversimplification, but mindfulness is in many ways the *opposite* of stress and anxiety. When we are anxious, we are usually unconscious, reactive, and behaving automatically. When we are mindful, we instantly achieve that distance from perception that awareness brings, we allow ourselves to *choose* our response (if any), and maybe even have the opportunity to leave behind old patterns once and for all.

Meditation for Novices and Veterans

We already know that mindfulness is not the same as meditation, but for most purposes, it's useful and convenient to think about mindfulness in terms of a meditation practice. To define it simply, **meditation is any mental practice involving three key features: awareness, focus, and relaxation.** Though we can find these three experiences in a range of different activities, meditation is the *deliberate pursuit of all three.*

Usually done quietly and alone in a seated position, with eyes closed, we can expand meditation to include the more popular, psychology-based perspective, wherein we become more familiar with our inner cognitive and psychological processes. This means we can use meditation to become more aware of and skilled at things like concentrating or observing neutrally without attachment.

This definition may sound simple, but due to its intangible and personal nature, meditation has often been misunderstood, and myths abound about what counts as meditation. First, don't believe that you need to wear certain clothes, burn incense, sit on a special cushion or play whale song in the background. The only requirement is that you are still and undisturbed— although that doesn't mean you can't meditate if there are dogs barking in the distance or noisy neighbors upstairs!

You don't need to be a Buddhist or include any particular religious or spiritual elements in your meditation practice— unless you want to, of course. There are people who will go to great lengths to make meditation seem like a very exclusive club, or suggest that you need decades of practice before you can even be considered a beginner. This is nothing more than ego.

In fact, many of the myths associated with meditation are ego-based. In truth, there's no need to make any grand changes to your identity just because you practice meditation. You are not betraying your chosen religion or committing to a life of an ascetic monk or a new-age spiritualist. You're just meditating, and *anyone* can meditate. You don't need a master or a guru, or to attend a month-long retreat that costs you thousands (although, again, there's nothing to stop you doing these things if you want to).

Some people look at meditation and see nothing but avoidance—it seems selfish to them, to sit around doing "nothing" while there's real work to be done. By the time you're done reading this book, you'll hopefully see that meditation is one of the most valuable ways to spend your time, and, rather than being escapist and selfish, it actually encourages an embracing of reality and a deep compassion for self and others.

Though meditation can lead to relaxation, it is *not* the same as simply chilling out (as valuable as chilling out is!). Relaxation is an effect of meditation, but not strictly its method. Similarly, using affirmations, visualizations, trance, or self-hypnosis may be beneficial, but these things encourage a wholly different state of mind than does meditation. There are many different states of consciousness—to simply alter consciousness (for example, through psychedelics) is not the same as meditation.

Finally, though meditation is not effortless (after all, you are trying to focus and concentrate on the present moment, which is by definition effortful), it is not in itself difficult. You are not meant to be fighting against yourself or forcing your mind to clear. Yes, the process can seem daunting/boring/confusing to a beginner, but it's something anyone can do with practice—even those of us who feel we don't have the time or are more distractible than others.

As you learn more about what meditation is and how it feels, you may encounter your own biases and misconceptions about it. Try to keep an open mind, though, and be receptive to learning more.

Mindfulness is not Synonymous with Meditation

We've already seen that mindfulness and meditation are not exactly the same thing. But if there are so many benefits to simply being more mindful, what's the point of taking up meditation as well? Though experts and gurus of all stripes have debated the issues extensively, the truth is probably that they are two overlapping and complimentary paths to well-being.

Mindfulness is a state of awareness, which can be cultivated using the technique or practice of meditation. However, some people claim that meditation is an umbrella term that encompasses mindfulness, itself a form of meditation, along with other forms like yoga, tantra, mindful breathing, contemplating emptiness, visualization, etc.

Being mindful, we bring our full attention and awareness to a single thing—the present moment or our breath, for example. Though mindfulness can be used during meditation, meditation can employ a range of other techniques and work toward a variety of different ends. Mindfulness is a little like the ability to run, whereas meditation encompasses all the different forms of sports—many of which require running.

Why meditate? Well, you don't have to. There are benefits to simply being more mindful. However, a meditation practice can take you a little further. Whether you want to tap into the deepest secrets of being itself and reach divine union, enlightenment, and the dissolution of your illusory ego, or you simply want to relax a little and be more emotionally balanced, meditation and mindfulness can help depending on how they're used. Because this is a book about overthinking, you can probably guess that we're looking at ways to use meditation to cut short the root of so much anxiety—i.e. mental chatter.

Types of Meditation—Which Would Work Best for You?

So that leads us to the next obvious question—which type of meditation should you practice?

It's not enough to simply sit cross-legged, close your eyes, and dive in with no sense of purpose or direction. It makes sense to choose an approach that actually fits *your* needs and goals.

To determine what those goals are, ask yourself: what's missing from your life right now?

How are you in general—how is your body, how is your mind? Do you have tense muscles, overactive, racing thoughts, or trouble tempering your emotions?

What do you hope to really achieve from meditation—energy, focus, purpose, insight, healing?

Assessing where you are right now will help you better decide which form of meditation to pursue first. Most beginners usually benefit from a more secular, contemporary approach with clear goals and a structure to stick to. Some of these approaches include:

Guided Meditation

This is what it sounds like—there is a recorded voice or a live teacher who leads you through a structured meditation session. Typically, you will be asked to focus on either visualizations, or to concentrate on your breath or a part of your body as you relax. Guided meditations are often themed, and they can be great for beginners since they are a fixed length.

They're perfect for people just starting out who want to get the meditation ball rolling, and can improve well-being and focus, while building discipline with regular practice. This is a good place to start for those looking to lower anxiety and stress in general.

Loving-Kindness Meditation

In this meditation, you direct your conscious awareness to one specific aim: generating feelings of compassion and loving kindness toward yourself, others, and the world at large. This kind of meditation can be profoundly healing and completely change your world when done regularly. Improving not only social relationships but your ability to have self-compassion, this form of meditation is a great fit for people wanting to heal emotional wounds and cultivate empathy. If strong negative emotions, trauma, and bad memories are wrapped up in your anxiety, this kind of meditation may work wonders.

Mantra Meditation

It can be difficult and confusing for some to "concentrate on the moment" but more intuitive to dwell on a repeated, often meaningless spoken phrase to continually refocus the mind. Any sound or word, if repeated, can be a tool to gently anchor in the present, and it may be a wonderful way for some people to structure a meditation practice. If you've ever seen those monks, often depicted in the media, repeatedly saying "om" at regular intervals, then you have an idea of what mantra meditation looks like.

Mantra meditation is excellent for those of us who get carried away with ever-tightening anxiety loops or runaway self-talk. It's also great if you're a little doubtful of the whole meditation thing and the idea of "emptying the mind" seems as terrifying as it does impossible!

Breathing Meditation

The same effect can be achieved by using the breath. By staying with your breath, you stay in the moment and strengthen your mind-body connection—great for people who have difficulty with rumination and anxiety. Breathing meditation can be wonderfully grounding and can clear the mind. The breath, in its way, is a mantra— in and out, always the same. We'll be looking at deliberate grounding practices in the next chapter.

Mindfulness Meditation

Here, we consciously practice becoming aware of what emerges in our present reality without judgment or attachment. We stay in the moment, and when we become aware of our attention wandering to the past or the future, or into a mental story, we calmly release it and come back to the present instead. This kind of meditation increases focus and decreases emotional reactivity, helping us gain a deeper sense of awareness and self-regulation. This is great for blending in with CBT approaches or journaling, as it strengthens your ability to stop, put distance between yourself and anxious ruminations, and calmly decide if you *want* to pursue any train of thought. You may need to set a timer to remind you when your session is over.

A Mindful Framework

Mindfulness meditation is a popular and wonderful practice to choose as a beginner. You may be tempted to jump right in and start straight away, but take the time to lay the groundwork before beginning in earnest—this way you're less likely to get disheartened, bored, or irritated and stop before you've had the chance to progress.

First, decide *when* you'll practice. It's best to have a routine. Any time will work as long as it's a time of day where you're relatively free of distractions and can devote time and energy to practice. Ten minutes at first is more than enough, and you can practice after a daily exercise or yoga routine.

Next, decide *where* you'll practice. You don't need over-the-top hippie décor—you just need a peaceful, quiet place away from distractions. Set your timer, switch off your phone, tell people in your household you'll need some time to yourself, and then start. If it helps, a little yoga to warm up can get you in the right frame of mind, as can a gentle walk, a journal session, a little prayer or ritual, or even some light music.

When you're ready, find your seated position—stable but not straining. There's no need for a super erect, uncomfortable posture. On the floor or in a chair is great. Settle in for a moment, finding comfort and balance. Keep your upper arms parallel to the rest of your body, palms on your upper thighs (no need for hand positions). Keep your chin slightly lowered, eyes closed or gaze gently downward without any focus.

Now, be there. Relax. Become aware of your breath and follow it as it moves in and out of your body. Feel the slight friction of the air as it enters your nostrils. Note the soft rise of your chest, the warmth of the breath, the silence in your ears.

Whether it's within a single second or it takes five minutes, your mind will likely wander. Your awareness may jump to an unanswered email, to an event that happened yesterday morning, to the hunger in your stomach, to a vague feeling of apprehension floating around your lower belly . . . that's okay. Let it go and come back to the breath, to the present.

Rather than an attitude of judgment, have a little moment of gratitude that you came back to the moment, then let that gratitude go as well. It's all grist for the mill. If you feel an itch, pause and put your awareness there. Withhold scratching it or readjusting yourself. Can you just stay with the sensation as it is? You'll probably see this as a chance to develop mental and emotional resilience, as well as distress tolerance—what's an itch, really? Doesn't it just pass eventually, like any anxious thought?

When you're done, come out of meditation slowly and gently. Reconnect to your environment and notice how you feel inside and out. Don't just jump back into the day—reflect on *how* you'd like to continue. The more you practice, the more you will start to see the boundary between meditating and not meditating disappear.

This general meditation approach can be combined with any of the techniques discussed in previous chapters. For example, you could commit to a daily habit of waking up to do meditation first thing in the morning. Then, after ten minutes or so, you can sit down with a journal to note down five things you're grateful for, as well as making notes or lists to help you examine the anxieties floating around in your head so you can postpone them for later. You'll start the morning feeling calmer, more in control, and more aware of what you're doing moment to moment.

Be careful about turning your meditation practice into a new source of anxiety. Don't beat yourself up about doing things wrong. There's no need for competitiveness, judgment, shame, or pride. (Although, if you notice yourself doing any of this, great! It's the noticing that matters.)

Things to Keep in Mind about Meditation

It bears repeating—you don't need to *buy* anything to begin meditating. Not a special cushion, not bells or worry beads, not a fancy course or retreat or app. The only one hundred percent necessary thing is you and the present moment—which you already have!

Keep in mind that the goal is not to empty your head entirely, and that wandering thoughts are not a sign that you're weak or out of practice or doing it wrong. In fact, this is exactly what mindfulness meditation feels like. Embrace the present without judgment—*all* of the present, whatever it looks like. Even if the present is just you judging yourself, or you being distracted and tired. Even if it's just your brain wondering when you'll give it something more interesting to do.

Gravity isn't an enemy of your workout, and likewise your brain wandering around isn't an enemy of your meditation practice. It's just what brains do. But you are not your brain alone.

It's okay to not enjoy the occasional practice, to feel frustrated, or to feel like you're not "progressing." But to help yourself out, don't try to meditate when you're physically, mentally, or emotionally exhausted. Don't meditate with a full belly. Wear clothing that is comfortable, and make sure that no devices are beeping or chiming during your session.

Challenges and Obstacles with Mental Chatter

It's perfectly normal for things not to go quite according to plan at first. Don't let a little snag in the beginning convince you that you're not cut out for meditation, and stop entirely. You may just need to do some troubleshooting.

First, don't worry if you're shocked by just how uncontrollable and unruly your mind is! Don't freak out and attempt to *stop* these thoughts—remember, your only goal is to notice, without judgment or interpretation. Whenever you become aware, you are strengthening that muscle. It doesn't matter how many times you falter then become aware and come back to the moment.

Being caught up in a frenzied mess of thoughts can feel like a seductive trance you can't help but slip into. But when you do, just slip out of it again. Watch and see that even though thoughts come, they also fade away. You're not doing anything wrong. Your brain is just doing its thing, but that doesn't mean you have to go along for the ride. What happens if you just sit back a little and watch it all unfold? In other words, can you let stress and anxiety happen without getting stressed and anxious about it? (Sorry to get all Mr. Miyagi on you there.)

Notice the planning, fantasizing, worrying, analyzing, interpreting, storytelling, judging, questioning . . . Just be there and be aware of it.

Notice if you are grasping at something, wanting to be somewhere other than the moment, wanting to escape or deny what's in front of you. Notice how you may push certain sensations away in anger or fear, or jump toward others to cling to them in desperation or excitement. Watch to see if you feel sleepy, irritable, restless, or doubtful. Are you asking yourself, "Is this even working?"

A great way to approach all these challenges is not to see them as problems at all. They're simply part of the experience; a universal human experience. What happens when you *don't* try to control, resist, or judge? Your attention can go to what is arising without identifying with it. You can name it—fear, anger—without getting lost in it or stuck in its thought spirals.

A key principle to keep in mind is that you are not your thoughts. Any thought could occur in your mind, but it does not follow that you have to believe every thought you think, or that you have to act on every idea that floats in your head. When a thought comes, you can simply stand aside and observe as it passes by, as if watching a cloud float across the otherwise blue skies. As you master the art of beholding your thoughts in this way, you are saved from being carried away by destructive urges and emotions. You become better at simply letting things be instead of trying to control or judge everything that happens to you. **You get to meet all experiences with compassionate attention. Then you are able to let them go.**

If you have experienced a great trauma, it may not be advisable initially to stay with very intense or powerful emotions as they emerge. Some traumas are so severe that they evoke emotions unmanageable by meditative practices alone. Such adverse experiences need to be processed through trauma work with a trained mental health professional before you can safely hold these emotions by yourself.

If for any reason you begin to feel intensely uncomfortable or overwhelmed by emotions during meditation, it may make more sense to place attention on something calming and compassionate instead of staying with the emotion. If you feel like you may be descending into panic or becoming disconnected from your body, anchor into the present moment using the 5-4-3-2-1 grounding technique: Look around you and identify five things that you see, four things that you feel, three things that you hear, two things that you smell, and one thing that you taste (or if you find this difficult, one good thing about yourself).

Mindfulness meditation is about full, open awareness—but be patient and compassionate with yourself. It sometimes takes time to bear witness to emotions, memories, sensations, thoughts, or parts of ourselves that are distressing. Focus awareness on a soothing image, a person you love, or a mantra that reaffirms your safety and well-being.

Finally, what about all those more mundane distractions—i.e. that wildly annoying feeling of your legs going to sleep, or a tiny mosquito buzzing around your ears?

The sad fact is, most of us are not used to sitting up straight unsupported. Cramps, itching, and numbness might happen. On the other hand, previously ignored sensations may come flooding to the fore. In the past, you might have been able to push away such sensations because you've been operating on autopilot and often get powered up by adrenaline in these busy times. However, now that you inject mindfulness in your life and take time to be still and observe, a heightened awareness of your body can make you aware of just how tired or unwell you feel.

Here's the trick: *any* sensation, be it mental, emotional, physical, or spiritual, can be dealt with in the same way: with compassionate awareness. We can sit with and accept unpleasant physical sensations just as we can emotional or mental ones. Just offer gentle attention. Breathe into it.

Be kind to yourself and open up a space to experience what you are experiencing. Notice what springs up in you in response to a physical sensation—can you see a whole cascade of inner thoughts and feelings that erupt over a simple leg itch?

Meet these with kindness and non-attachment, too.

You could direct your attention to something else if physical discomfort is really weighing on you. Be present with the feeling of unpleasantness—try not to immediately flee the sensation (but then again, there's nothing wrong with "giving up" and shifting position, or ending the session). Just remind yourself that all these sensations are fleeting. Put a little distance between you and doubt, discomfort, or rumination. Discomfort in a part of your body or doubt entering your mind are all part of you, but they are not you—hence, you can retain a consciousness that is not bothered or irritated by these sensations, but one that is able to hold and accept them as they come.

The Most Probable Culprits of Meditation Troubles

There's nothing wrong with experiencing worry, rage, irritation, doubt, lack of motivation, restlessness, impatience, low mood, or even falling asleep while you try to meditate. It's normal to get carried away with planning something else, trying too hard and getting frustrated, or finding it impossible to care enough to stick with it.

That being said, there are a lot of meditation mistakes that will make it so much more likely that you'll experience these kinds of challenges.

The most common is simple: your practice is not consistent. Strive to be consistent with meditating daily. You don't need to worry about allotting a huge chunk of your day to sitting on the floor and closing your eyes as you immerse yourself in meditative practice. The length of time you sit is of secondary importance to the regularity of your practice. Your mind is churning around constantly, twenty-four-seven. For a meditation practice to have any noticeable effect, it needs to be frequent enough to make a difference. Knowing this, have some discipline. If your day is jam-packed with task after task on your to-do list, sit for only two or three minutes—it's better than nothing.

Practice with commitment and intention. Have respect for yourself and your practice, and give it the time and intensity it deserves—sloppiness or lack of effort is a disservice to yourself. Meditation is not just some boring thing on your to-do list, so don't treat it like one! Prepare well before each session and give it the care and consideration it deserves. Set your intention, take some breaths, and ease into it.

Related to this is simply expecting too much, too soon. It took you a lifetime to be what you are right now—you will not magically achieve radical changes within a few weeks. Most of us begin a practice because of the benefits. Hard as it is, though, try to forget these in the moment and practice simply for its own sake. No grasping. Forget about the end result. Pay attention to how it feels to meditate in each passing second, and nothing more. As with exercise that ultimately becomes a more enjoyable experience when you're fully in the moment, relishing how your body feels as you stretch and work your muscles, so does meditation become totally gratifying when you surrender yourself to the experience.

If you are too impatient for quick results, you may be tempted to flit from one technique to another, confusing yourself and never giving any one method a chance to work. Experimentation is great, but be modest in your expectations. No meditation session, no matter what technique you use, can radically alter your life as a whole with a single go. Give a new routine a good few weeks before deciding it isn't for you.

Low self-esteem and doubt can be a particularly pernicious obstacle to meditation. You may overanalyze and wonder if you're doing it right, becoming self-conscious rather than self-aware! Appraising the meditation process as it happens actually just takes you out of the moment and ultimately demotivates you.

To overcome this, remind yourself that it's okay to be on a learning curve. Just keep going—more familiarity and clarity will come with time. It's okay to be uncertain, or to make mistakes. Nobody is watching or judging you! Ask questions, keep learning, and don't worry about doing it perfectly. If you can bring your mind back after it wanders—then don't worry, you're doing it right.

Be kind to yourself and don't beat yourself up if you miss a session or have a "bad" session. Self-criticism is only another distraction—mindfully and compassionately let it go.

Finally, there may be a bunch of things you routinely do outside of meditation that actually interfere with your attempts. Allowing your mind to spin out of control throughout the rest of the day is going to make meditation much harder. You can't undo a day's worth of binge-drinking and junk food with ten minutes at the gym, and you can't counteract a day of chaos and stress with a ten-minute mindfulness session, no matter how relaxing.

Is your life disorganized, erratic, or bursting with emotional volatility? Do you constantly fill your mind with noise—news, social media, movies, gaming, internet? Information overload can be so intense it takes an entire meditation session just to come down off the dopamine high. Do you engage in bad habits that undermine your overall health, like under-sleeping, never exercising, or drinking too much coffee?

Meditation is great, but it's not a magical mind vitamin that will cancel out a terrible daily diet of mindless information consumption and unhealthy habits. The more your non-meditating life is in alignment with your meditating one, the more results you'll see.

In this vein, let's briefly mention not just the quantity of information you're bombarding your nervous system with daily, but its *quality*. Unfortunately, much of the noise we encounter on social media, in the news and online, in TV and movies, and (perhaps worst of all) in advertising is deliberately designed to capture our attention by force and hold it hostage.

Flashy, emotive, and hard to look away from, these images and words affect us deeply, cognitively, and emotionally, not to mention they actively instigate feelings of desire, craving, strong emotions, distraction, and addiction.

A little mindfulness in our media consumption can do wonders. Simply notice what you're feeding your brain day in and day out. What effect is it really having to read that rage-inducing article online, to watch that depressing documentary, or to engage in the Instagram scrolling that leaves you feeling utterly worthless as a human being?

A "media detox" can help you calm down, recenter, and take charge of your own awareness again, not to mention boosting self-regulation and saving you a bunch of wasted time. Put mindful limits on what you consume, how, why, how often, and for how long. This may be as simple as deciding you will not start every day by reaching for your phone within seconds of waking up.

How to Address Meditation Challenges

If you're encountering constant mental chatter, remind yourself: it's not a problem.

Thinking is what brains do. You're not trying to eliminate thoughts, just become aware of them, and in doing so, find space and distance. The trick is that resisting and avoiding is simply more of the same—so don't resist. Just notice.

This is what it really means to have an attitude of compassionate acceptance—to not cling to some idea of how you should be, but to simply welcome what is. Are you feeling restless and agitated? Okay. That's how you are right now. Sit with that. Has a strong emotion emerged within you? Okay. It's no less worthy of your kind attention than any other sensation.

When you stop resisting, you'll notice something interesting—things flow. It's the grasping or pushing against certain sensations that makes meditation feel difficult and conflict-ridden. When we let go, we see that there is no need to control or force or prevent or cultivate anything. The present moment is just right exactly as it is.

And it changes! Anger, sadness, or restless legs don't seem like such a big deal when you notice that they are never permanent, but rise and fall in the moment, like waves, disappearing just as they arrived. Go deeper and watch how your consciousness itself is also moving and changing over time.

In the beginning, impediments to meditation may seem big and obvious, but they become more subtle the more you practice. You may notice yourself getting up after a session feeling slightly disappointed, perturbed by an unconscious desire to achieve . . . something. A state of bliss, a happy flash of insight, or some deep calm as your reward for being so disciplined?

Again, these sensations are just waves in the ocean. In time, you may start to see that awareness is its own reward, that the present moment is sufficient in itself, and that all you can ever really do is be who you already are, in the ever-unfolding, perfectly formed, peaceful moment.

Making Meditation a Learned Habit

Researchers from the University College London have found that it takes around sixty-six days for a habit to become cemented, or, as they put it, for a person to develop "automaticity." That said, there also seems to be large variation between individuals—some participants took as little as eighteen days, while others took a whopping 254 days. Naturally, the kind of habit in question also determines how easy it is to adopt in the long term.

How long does it take for meditation to become a fixed habit? There's no telling. But committing to regular practice in the beginning is far more important than trying to tough out super-long sessions before you've properly established a habit.

To help your new meditation habit really stick, there are a few simple but powerful tricks you can use; for example, "habit anchoring." Choose a thirty-second activity that will prompt you to meditate—like stretching, counting breaths, or saying a mantra—and then connect this thirty seconds to an established habit you already have, such as getting out of the shower, waking up, or making your morning cup of coffee.

This way, you tack on a new habit to an old one by way of a smaller activity that will kickstart your momentum. For example, you always have your bedtime routine, but now you're reminding yourself to do a quick stretch beforehand, which leads you into a ten-minute loving-kindness meditation practice.

The "habit loop formula" is a related idea. A loop consists of a cue, a reward, and a craving, and to establish a new routine (such as a morning meditation practice), you'll need all three.

A cue is something that triggers behavior; for example, you waking up in the morning. A reward is a benefit for doing the behavior, such as feeling calm and centered after a morning meditation practice.

Finally, craving refers to the urge you feel when your brain *associates these two*— connecting the cue with the expected reward, i.e. when you wake up, your brain associates meditation with beneficial feelings of calm, which it then craves.

By deliberately strengthening the association of the cue and the feelings of reward, you anchor the behavior. Do this by mentally conjuring up the positive benefits of meditation every time you experience your cue, and thus cement in your mind the fact that you enjoy and crave meditation. The process won't be automatic at first, but every time you follow through, you strengthen those loops and take one step closer to an automatic habit.

Make sure your environment supports your habit by giving yourself time and space and reducing clutter, and be clear and honest about your true motivations for taking up a meditation practice—you'll need to tap into this deep motivation on tired or lazy days when you don't feel like meditating! Choose a meditation style you actually like and hold yourself accountable. Give yourself a little reward once you complete each session, or track your progress so you can see your self-discipline strengthening with time.

Most importantly, just keep going! Expect that it won't be easy to start a new daily habit, whatever it is. Don't be discouraged if you slip up; just get back into your routine as soon as you can. A skipped session or a difficult time isn't a sign that something is going wrong—but coming back to your practice no matter what is proof that you're strengthening your resolve, committing to your well-being, and giving yourself the opportunity to really develop.

Summary

- Meditation is the deliberate and consistent cultivation of awareness, focus, and relaxation.
- Some widespread notions about meditation are nothing but myths. You don't need to convert to Buddhism or even incorporate religious elements in your practice. Meditation is not selfish avoidance of reality; rather, it cultivates full acceptance of reality. Meditation also does not require fighting with yourself just to keep your mind clear.
- While mindfulness is generally taken to be a state that can be fostered through the practice of meditation, some people consider mindfulness as itself a form of meditation, along with other forms such as yoga, tantra, and visualization.
- There are many different types of meditation, and you can practice the one you resonate most with. Guided

meditation involves a recorded voice or live teacher leading a structured meditation session. Loving-kindness meditation trains you to yield your conscious awareness toward developing self-compassion. Mantra meditation has you speak out a repeated or meaningless word or sound to anchor you in the present. In breathing meditation, you focus on your breath in order to stay in the moment. Mindfulness meditation involves a conscious practice of nonjudgment and non-attachment while cultivating awareness of the present.

- It's best to have a routine as to when and where you meditate. Choose a time and place where you're relatively free from distractions. Most important is that your practice is consistent and that you approach it with a willingness to meet each moment with calm, kind awareness.

- Among the most common challenges in meditation are lack of consistency; expecting too much; impatience; low self-esteem and doubt; and an out-of-control, racing mind resulting from a highly stimulating day with a lot of stresses and unhealthy habits.

- It will take time to make meditation a habit, but you can help it along by attaching it to other daily habits you already have. Habit anchoring, a technique wherein you designate a thirty-second activity as a prompt for your meditation practice, helps you incorporate meditation more easily in your daily life. You can also employ the habit loop formula, which consists of a cue, a reward, and a craving as elements of establishing a new routine.

Chapter 5. De-stress for a New You

Our final chapter is all about what you do when you're *not* meditating. Anxiety is a way of life, and so is serenity and calm, conscious control.

But just as distress is a normal and unavoidable part of life, so is a certain amount of stress and worry. Life would be impossibly boring and meaningless without it! Even people without full-blown anxiety disorders or problems with overthinking can have lives that are overrun with stress. Stress is like weeds in the garden—if you don't pull them up when they're small, they grow big quickly and soon take over everything (i.e. become an anxiety disorder, burnout, or physical illness).

Rather than waiting for stress to pile up and manifest as a Big Problem, we can decide to make a habit of releasing tension and stress daily, even moment by moment. In the very beginning of this book, we saw how trying to control what you don't really have control over is hopeless, and how trying to avoid distress or uncertainty actually only makes things worse. But there is something you actually *do* have control over—your daily habits, your routines, your regular mental health practices and self-care. And this is more than enough!

Our main goal in de-stressing is to pinpoint exactly what is going on in our heads when we overthink. It's about identifying the triggers that set us off as well as the effects of that overthinking once it begins. When we can see the process clearly, we can then begin to take informed action. But the necessary starting point? Awareness.

In this chapter, we'll begin with the basics of overcoming overthinking and managing your stress levels, but in each case, what is most important is that we maintain an *awareness* of ourselves. Awareness is not rumination, though: when we are aware, we simply turn our attention onto both our inner and outer experience, without judgment, and without clinging or resisting. We can cultivate this awareness in ourselves by regularly "checking in" with our bodily sensations, thoughts, and feelings by making sure that our lifestyle is supporting us in the ways we need it to, and by including some form of mindfulness in everyday life.

It's the end of a long day and you're exhausted. You were late for the morning meeting and had an argument with a colleague. You were given too much work again. The builders outside have been making noise *all day long* and driving you crazy. Your to-do list is as long as you are, and you feel close to the breaking point, when your boyfriend sends you a cryptic message saying you "need to talk." Suddenly, it's like a rumination and overthinking tap is turned on and your head floods with anxious thoughts, worries, and catastrophic predictions.

When stress piles on in this way, it can feel utterly overwhelming. It's like playing an ultra-fast game of Tetris, where you can't think straight because there's always another challenge, another crisis demanding your attention. Even though it can often feel like there's nothing you can do about stress (that thought alone is stressful!), there are always ways to stop, take a breath, and notice what's happening.

The Four A's of Stress Management

This technique can be like a lifeboat in the storm of stress and overthinking. It's easier to get into than meditation and will help you get a handle on everyday life stressors fast. All you need to remember is four techniques: **avoid, alter, accept, and adapt**. It can be a comfort in itself to know that really, there are only these four possible ways to respond to any life stress. If you can, write them down somewhere you can see them at a glance until you've drilled it into your mind and can remember it instantly.

The first thing you can do is **avoid**.

Sounds suspiciously simple, but there's a lot of aggravation in life you can simply walk away from. We can't control everything in life, but we can arrange our circumstances so that we don't have to be in stressful surroundings or with stressful people. If we're honest, we might see that a lot of the stress in our lives is voluntary—and we don't have to agree to it!

Think about what is stressing you in your environment and how you can take control to moderate or remove it entirely. Consider someone who hates how busy the grocery stores are on Saturday morning. Knowing that this stresses them out, they can rearrange their schedule so they do their weekly shopping at the quietest time, say, on a Tuesday evening. There's no need to manage the stress of a busy supermarket if you just avoid it entirely.

You can avoid stressful people in exactly the same way. Do you find that your stress goes through the roof when your parents come to stay for the holidays? Find a way to have them stay in a nearby B&B, or avoid planning any activities where you are all alone together in a room for hours with nothing to do but stress each other out.

When you avoid stress, you are not running away from obligations or denying genuine problems. You are simply learning to say "no" to stress that is unnecessary and harmful. We can always say no to situations and people that demand too much of us and our resources. Those resources can be mental energy and attention, but they can also be time. If something in your life is gobbling up all your time, you *can* say no.

Look at your to-do list and get rid of the two or three items that are not urgent and not your priority. Delegate tasks, or let someone else take on a responsibility. You don't have to do it all! So, the next time you face a stressful prospect, ask yourself, "Can I just avoid this whole thing?" If you can, do it. This is not only a big step to creating healthy boundaries, it's a way of simplifying and streamlining life and getting in touch with your guiding values. So much of our anxiety and stress comes from areas of life we don't even care about if we're honest. Why waste your sense of balance and well-being on something that doesn't ultimately matter or mean anything to you?

If you can't avoid the situation, you might need to find ways to change it, i.e. **alter** it.

You always have the option of asking others to change their behavior. For example, if the builders are making a racket outside, politely ask them to pause for ten minutes while you finish an important phone call. Communicate your needs and feelings directly, rather than suffering in silence. If you never clearly tell your friend that his stupid jokes really hurt you, you may sit quietly and bear the brunt of it forever, when it would have been easy to tell him how you feel and ask him to stop.

We can't avoid every stress in life, but we often have a say in how these events unfold. Talk to people, negotiate, and use "I" statements to share your needs and ask for what you want. If you can't help but go to the store on Saturday morning, play your audiobook on your phone and listen to it while you shop if it relaxes you. If you can't avoid that extra PTA meeting, try to lump it in with other errands you're already doing so you save time, effort, and potentially gas for your car. You can also do a lot to alter unavoidable situations by cutting them down to a more manageable size. If you can't get out of going to that boring party, go but be upfront in the beginning and say, "Unfortunately I have to go in an hour—early start tomorrow!"

In meditation, we watch stressful and anxious thoughts as they arise and consciously choose our response to them. But with careful avoidance and management, we can actually step in and tweak our lives so that stressful thoughts don't get as much chance to appear in the first place. We can engineer a lifestyle that is in itself minimally stressful—or at least make sure that what stress remains is genuinely worth it.

Basically, if you can't avoid a stressor, ask what you can do to change it.

If your answer is "not much," then you might need to go one step further and **accept** it.

How do you accept a situation you dislike? First, if you dislike it, then you dislike it. Acceptance doesn't mean pretending you don't feel how you feel; it's an acknowledgment that it's *okay* to feel that way. Validate your own emotions and own them. For example, your boyfriend has just broken up with you via text, and there's not much you can do about his decision. But you can work on accepting the situation by calling up a friend to share your feelings.

If the situation is one in which you've been wronged, acceptance may take the form of trying to find a way to forgive. Remember that forgiveness is something you do for yourself and not the other person. When you forgive, you are releasing yourself from the stress and energy of resenting and blaming the other person.

Acceptance may also be about the subtle shifts in the way we frame events. We can't change the events themselves, but we can watch how we talk about them inwardly and the language we use. For example, instead of saying, "I completely failed my course and wasted my money. I'm such an idiot for not working harder," you could say, "I made a mistake and I'm not happy about it. But this one event doesn't define me. I can learn from mistakes and move on. I can do better next time."

Acceptance doesn't mean we agree with what happened or that we like it and shouldn't try to change it. It only means we gracefully come to terms with what we can't realistically change so we can focus on what we can. This step can be a powerful tool for overcoming the kind of anxiety that comes with resentment, or bitter recollection of things that have happened long in the past. Regrets and wishing how things could have, should have, might have been are a big recipe for anxiety. But acceptance diffuses and softens that anxiety and allows you to realize that it cannot be changed.

In the longer term, we do our best in the face of stress if we can **adapt**. Adapting means making more lasting changes to our worldview, our goals, our perception, and our expectations. Picture someone who is a perfectionist and is always stressed out because they never seem to meet their high standards. The best approach isn't that they find a way to be Superman, but instead lower their expectations so they're more reasonable and in line with reality. They have not magically found a way to completely overhaul their reality, but instead adapted to that reality and evolved into a form that's better suited to it.

Adapting to stress means we change *ourselves* to better cope with life. You might simply refuse to engage in depressing thoughts and deliberately practice being a person who is more optimistic. When we alter our perspective, we can see things differently. Is this a "crisis" or a "challenge"? How does this obstacle look when we tell ourselves, "I'm a resilient person," compared to when we tell ourselves, "Life isn't fair. This will end badly like everything does."?

When we adapt to stress, we find ways to make ourselves stronger. We build a worldview for ourselves that empowers us. For example, someone might get into the habit of making a "gratitude list" every day of all the wonderful things they are actually blessed with in life. Another person might meditate on their own personal "code" or say a mantra daily to remind them that they are strong and they can get through adversity. If we have an arsenal of powerful attitudes, ideas, philosophies, and inspiration, we can go into the world knowing that we can handle stress—and maybe even be better people for it!

With time, practicing meditation can achieve some of these core level changes and genuinely alter how we see ourselves and the world. But any time we are actively and consciously engaging with meaning, we are building our own characters and our own vision of who we are as people. You might see yourself today as someone who is hounded by anxiety. But there is also strength in realizing that you have other amazing qualities, too—diligence, kindness, intelligence, creativity, humor. And all of these can help you frame and offset anxiety.

So, those are the four A's of stress management. When you find yourself feeling anxious, pause and run through each of them in sequence. No matter how stressful the situation, there is a way for you to engage with it mindfully and proactively. You are not helpless in the face of stress—you have tools at your disposal! To use these tools, all it takes is a little awareness.

For example, there may be a colleague at work who stresses you out daily. Instead of getting overwhelmed by telling yourself there's nothing you can do about it, pause and ask if you can simply *avoid* this colleague. Maybe you can have lunch at a different time to avoid meeting them in the cafeteria, or maybe you can physically move to work farther away from them. But let's say you can't avoid encountering them in weekly meetings, and this is where they frequently interrupt you or steal your ideas.

You think of ways to *alter* the situation. Can you get out of these meetings? Can you speak to your colleague privately and share your concerns ("I'm uncomfortable in meetings lately, and I feel dismissed when you interrupt me")? Can you speak up in meetings and assert a stronger boundary when you talk? If none of these are really possible, you can still *accept* the situation to some degree. You might confide in a close friend about your frustrations, or come to realize that this colleague actually interrupts everyone, so you won't continue to take it personally or let it stress you.

Finally, you can adapt by working on becoming an overall more confident and assertive person. When you genuinely feel that you have as much right to speak as anyone else, then you may feel more confident saying, "Sorry, I was still speaking," and carrying on calmly. Instead of stewing over what you *should* have said that evening, you have simply said it and moved on.

Stress Diaries and Journals

Another concrete way to bring more awareness to your daily experience of stress is to write it all down. With overthinking, it can sometimes seem like there are a million things on your plate at once, and it's hard to decide what single cause is really behind your anxiety. A stress diary can help you pinpoint your triggers and your reaction to them. From there, you can start taking active steps to managing your stress levels.

A stress diary is simply a written record of your level of stress and the accompanying information, which you can analyze later and use to take steps to manage stress. We all need some stress in life, so this diary can help us identify our optimal range.

The idea is simple: for each entry, record the time and date and how you're feeling right now. A common way to do this is on a rating scale (for example, one for not stressed at all and ten for super stressed), but you can also use feeling words or note physical symptoms (like sweaty palms). Also note how effective and productive you're feeling, using a scale as well. Then, note any stressful events that have recently happened as well as any ideas for what you feel could be the causes of your current state. Finally, note how you responded to the event and what the overall outcome was. For example:

4 February, 9:15

Received a worrying message about Dad needing surgery on his shoulder. Feeling around 4/10, kind of apprehensive and a little tired. Weird knot feeling in my stomach. Trouble staying focused on work: only working at about 1/10 effectiveness. I think I feel this way because I'm worried about something bad happening to him. I'm avoiding replying to the message, but I think this is making my anxiety worse.

Make an entry every time you feel your mood shifting, or when you're noticeably stressed. Keep a stress diary for a few days or a week, then sit down to analyze it and find any patterns:

1. What are the most frequent causes of stress, i.e. what usually comes before a sudden rise in stress or drop in mood?
2. How do these events typically affect your productivity?
3. How do you normally respond to these events, emotionally and behaviorally, and is your approach working?
4. Can you identify a level of stress that was comfortable and beneficial for your productivity?

When you analyze your stress diary like this, you are working with real data that can help you make insightful changes. You may even be surprised at some findings—only in writing things down in the moment do you see clear patterns emerge. You don't need to keep a stress diary forever. In fact, after using it a few weeks, the process might become automatic and you may develop more spontaneous awareness in the moment as stress is occurring.

Once you have a handle on the real causes of stress in your life, you can use something like the four A's technique to take action, or else rearrange your lifestyle or schedule to moderate stress. If you notice that all your stress is coming from one person, you can draw some boundaries around your relationship. If you notice that your normal response of getting angry tends to make things harder to handle, you can begin to work on your anger. If your job is a continued source of worry, you can gauge how bad it is and take action both short term (taking a holiday) or longer term (considering getting a different job).

The format described above isn't the only way that writing things down can help. You can keep a more traditional journal and explore your feelings more generally, whether occasionally or every day. Writing things down can relieve stress on its own, but it can also help you gather your thoughts, hash out problems, find insights, and process any issues you're going through. It's like your journal is an informal therapist!

Use journaling or diaries according to what you like and what works in your situation. If you're battling low mood and find your anxiety is general and seems to affect everything, you might find a gratitude journal helpful. Simply list five things daily that you are thankful for, even if it's nothing more exciting than your morning cup of coffee or the fact that you have a nice new pair of socks. This can subtly shift your focus onto your resources and possibilities, and reframe your experience.

If you are processing some traumatic life event or are going through a very difficult time, you might like to journal simply as an emotional release. "Dump" all your feelings onto paper and work through them. Once down on paper, you might start naturally gaining some self-knowledge or see some hints for ways forward. You could also combine this approach with worry postponement: schedule a fixed time in the future to tackle your worries in a journal and tell yourself that once you've put it down on paper, it's no longer in your mind.

If the stress in your life is more ongoing, you might like to try bullet journaling, where you use brief notes to keep track of daily goals, priorities, and memories. Keeping things brief can help you stay organized and add structure to your life. Some people like to bring an artistic element to bullet journaling and use color and pictures to express themselves and gather inspiration, encouraging positive feelings. Others use pre-made journals with prompts printed inside them.

Journals and diaries are not for everyone, though. Skip them if they only seem to make your perfectionism worse, or if you find yourself agonizing over the right technique. The journal is just a tool to get closer to your emotions—if you find yourself focusing more on the journal than your emotions, you might need to try a different technique. Try to finish every journaling session with something positive and grounding—recite a mantra, visualize something positive, or consider some possibilities and solutions going forward. If you don't make sure to return to a positive headspace, journaling may start to feel like it only encourages more unhappiness and overthinking.

The 5-4-3-2-1 Grounding Technique

Stress journals and the four A's technique can be used to great effect when paired together, especially if done regularly. But sometimes, you need a technique that will bring *immediate* relief to a stressful situation. The following technique is often used by those who experience panic attacks; it's a way to halt the "anxiety spiral" before it runs away with you. You don't have to have a panic disorder to benefit, though.

The idea is simple: when we overthink and ruminate and stress, we are *out of the moment*. We chew on thoughts of the past or entertain possibilities in the future. We think about "what if" and run our minds ragged on memories, ideas, probabilities, wishes, and fears. If we can pull our conscious awareness *back into the present,* we can halt some of this overthinking. And we can do this by checking in with the five senses. To put it another way, the brain can carry you all over the place, but the body—and its senses—is only ever one place: the present.

In moments of panic, we can get really caught up in ideas and thoughts, even though in reality, we are perfectly safe and sound and there is nothing in our immediate situation to threaten us. With panic, however, we can be sitting in perfect peace in a sunny garden somewhere and nevertheless feel like we're going to die. Such is the power of the mind!

The next time you feel anxiety and panic spiraling out of control, try this: stop, take a breath, and look around you.

• First, find five things in your environment that you can see. You might rest your eyes on the lamp in the corner, your own hands, a painting on the wall. Take a moment to really look at all these things; their textures, colors, shapes. Take your time to run your eyes over every inch and take it all in.

- Next, try to find four things in your environment that you can feel or touch. Feel the weight of your body against the chair, or the texture of the jacket you're wearing, or reach out to feel how cool and smooth the glass of the car window feels against your fingers.

- Next, find three things that you can hear. Your own breath. The distant sound of traffic or birds.

- Next, find two things you can smell. This might be tricky at first, but notice that everything has a smell if you pay attention. Can you smell the soap on your skin or the faint earthy smell of the paper on your desk?

- Finally, find one thing that you can taste. Maybe the lingering flavor of coffee on your tongue. Even if you can't find anything, just dwell for a moment on what your taste buds are sensing. Are they really "off" or does your mouth almost have a taste of its own when you stop to become aware of it? Stay there for a moment and explore that sensation.

The point of this exercise is, on the surface, distraction. While your senses are active, your brain is engaged in something other than endless rumination, and your overthinking is halted. You put a spanner in the works and stop runaway thoughts. Practice this technique often enough and you may notice that it instantly calms you and slows you down.

In the moment, you might not remember which sense comes next, but this isn't important. What matters is that you are giving your full and focused attention to something outside of yourself and letting anxious energy dissipate. It's difficult to stop a thought by saying, "I think I should stop thinking," because, obviously, this itself is a thought. But if you can put your brain on pause and re-engage your senses for a moment, you unhook yourself from the worry track and give yourself a moment to become present and calm.

If you are really feeling frazzled and can't be bothered trying to focus on a specific number of specific sensations, or if you're in a place where there genuinely isn't much to focus on, then defer to what's always with you: your breath. Just focus on that. Then, gradually, you can expand awareness to think of the sound of it, the physical sensation, and so on.

Narrative Therapy and Externalization

One more technique we'll consider comes from the world of narrative therapy, which explores the way that our lives are often construed as stories, or narratives. People are meaning-making machines, and we make meaning by telling stories about who we are and what the events of our lives signify. So much of our anxiety is a side effect from the stories that we are actively choosing to tell ourselves day in and day out. With narrative therapy, we can essentially rewrite these stories to find healing and, well, a happy ever after!

We've already discussed that a big part of overcoming anxiety is to look at our mental models and consciously make decisions about how we want to run our lives. When we are the narrator of our own stories, we take charge, reframe, and are empowered to make new meanings. The big tenet behind narrative therapy is that people are separate from their problems, and indeed, this idea underpins a popular technique called "externalization."

When we externalize, we put the problem *out there*. We are not wrong or bad to have problems, and we don't judge or blame ourselves for having them. Nevertheless, we do have the power to change how we talk about ourselves and our lives, and we can make meaningful changes. So, when it comes to overthinking, a big step is saying, "Overthinking is a problem, and I'm going to find alternatives," versus saying, "I am an overthinker and that's bad. I have to find a way to fix myself."

Another big step is to realize that you really are in control and are the *author* of your own experience—other people are not to blame for our perception, and equally they cannot save or teach us; we are the experts of our own experience. Can you see how this is the same as the difference between reactive and responsive, conscious and unconscious, purposeful and habitual?

Our mental models are a little like patterns or filters or repeating motifs. If your life was a movie, what genre would it be? What role would you always play, and how would the story play out? When we can see that our interpretations and frames influence our experience, we are empowered to change them for ourselves. For example, overthinkers tend to feel powerless, but what if they changed the story and saw themselves as being responsible and capable?

Let's return to externalization. You are not your problems. You are not your failures. If you can put distance between yourself and your life challenges, you gain perspective and untangle your sense of identity and self-worth from the temporary moment you're experiencing. Just like a cloud is not the sky, our problems are not who we are— they will pass, and we do have control over how we respond to them.

If you're feeling overwhelmed, it may help to repeat the mantra to yourself: "I am not my problems." Change your language, too. Instead of, "I'm an anxious person," say, "I'm experiencing anxiety right now," or even,

"I'm noticing some anxiety." We can put distance between ourselves and our problems in many ways:

- Use the journaling or stress diary techniques above. Take the anxiety out of your head and put it down on a piece of paper. Burn the paper or scrunch it up and throw it away. Physically see that the problem is separate from you, and from a distance, you can take action to change it.

- Use visualization and imagery. Visualize all the overthinking as air inside you that you blow into a giant balloon, and then imagine the balloon floating up and away from you, getting smaller and smaller. Really enjoy the sensation that you don't have to fully *identify* with your worries; you can put them down sometimes, and you can walk away to get perspective. Imagine the balloon disappearing out of sight, along with your worries. Another technique is to imagine yourself putting your worries away in a locked safe before going to bed. Tell yourself, "I can always open the safe and come and get these later if I want to, but for now, I'm sleeping."

- If you're inclined to, use creativity to externalize: write, draw, paint, or even sing and dance your problems, and make them real outside of your body. Some people give their judgmental or overly paranoid inner voice a name, so they can say, "Oh yes, this isn't *me*, that's just boring old Fred again, overthinking as usual. Hi, Fred!"

Another technique used in narrative therapy is deconstruction. When you overthink, the sensation is often one of overwhelm: there are a million things going on in your head, all at a thousand miles an hour, and you don't even know where to start with any of it. The great thing about a story, however, is that it's sequential. It's one step after another. If we're feeling lost in rumination, we can use story to help us break down (or deconstruct) a big, scary problem into smaller, easier ones.

A story is a way to organize, to slow things down, and to remind you that you are in control when it comes to where and how you place your attention. You cannot look at *everything* all at once. Trying to do so often makes you feel powerless and small in the face of overwhelming thoughts. But, as in any good story, you don't have to figure everything out immediately or solve every problem all at one time. Some ways to bring deconstruction into your own life:

- If things are feeling disastrous, stop and force yourself to focus on the *single thing* that is most important right now. If you're catastrophizing about things that may happen tomorrow or next year or whenever, set those aside and look at what matters today only, or perhaps only what matters in this very moment. Ask yourself, what single next step can you take? Don't worry about the next twenty steps, just take the next step you need to, and then you can go from there.

- If you find yourself returning to distressing memories from the past, take a moment to deliberately lay out your history, perhaps even writing it down or laying it out on a chart. Break down events into episodes and look for themes, patterns, and a thread that links them all together. See how the present moment ties into the past, then ask yourself what you can do to take charge of your own narrative. For example, if you're cringing over mistakes you made in the past, you might construct a story where you weren't just an idiot who did something wrong, but you were young and learning, and in your development, you're continually getting better. You can see that your embarrassment now is proof of you being a more mature person. You can see the *whole picture*— one of growth and progress. Doesn't that feel better than simply churning over a humiliating comment you made once in fifth grade?

- Anxiety and overthinking have a way of "fracturing" our attention and creating chaos and confusion. When we deconstruct all these thoughts, however, we see that many of them are just noise, and we don't necessarily have to entertain them. Maybe you're primarily concerned about your health, and off that single worry branches a million other thoughts of losing your job, of dying, expensive medical bills, etc. Deconstructing these means asking,

"What is this thought really about?" and distinguishing thoughts that derail and distract from those where you can actually make meaningful changes.

A Word on Ruminating

What does it mean to ruminate?

This word actually has a fascinating history: the word originates from the Latin term rūmināre, which literally means to chew over. This is why animals that "chew the cud" such as cows are called "ruminants." It's an apt way to describe a particular kind of thinking we all engage in from time to time. A cow ruminates by regurgitating partially digested material and re-chewing it, usually several times over. Mental rumination is just the same—we regurgitate old memories, ideas, and stale old themes to chew over again and again and again. But whereas chewing a cud is healthy and normal for a cow, rumination is seldom healthy and normal for a human!

Let's say you had a weird disagreement with a loved one and you keep playing the conversation over again in your mind.

Maybe you imagine you saying something else, or you're filled with regret or remorse. Something doesn't feel right about it all, so your brain keeps returning to the same scene, dwelling on it, putting a bright spotlight on every ugly detail, trying on different interpretations and hypothetical endings. Basically, rumination is overthinking.

It's chewing ideas down into a pulp, and it's unproductive. Often, we bring out an old memory that in turn triggers other (usually negative) memories, which catches us in a tightening loop of distraction and even more overthinking. You're chewing and chewing, but your problem-solving capacity is only getting worse, and your anxiety is rising. In other words, you can't stop telling yourself a really bad fairy tale over and over.

If you're a fan of dredging up bad memories from the past, the first step to stopping is to identify your triggers. Maybe it's going back home and seeing your old room. Maybe it's a certain song or a kind of food or the experience of being assessed. Whatever it is, you need to know what effect it has on you so you can act. The second step is to understand the form your rumination takes. Do you dwell on regret? Resentment? Despair? Do you blame others continually or beat yourself up with guilt?

Next, understand that you need both *awareness* and *distance* from this tired old rerun of a story that may have never even been accurate in the first place. In reading the previous techniques and approaches, this should be familiar to you by now. Psychologically take a step back from this story that seems to just run on its own once triggered. As in all the previous mindfulness exercises, simply observe it unfolding without identifying with it, attaching to it, or resisting it.

One way to gain distance is by **labeling**. Give the story a name. You could think, "Oh, here's *The Saga* again," anytime you recognize yourself being triggered into the same old tale of blame and anger. You can gain distance simply by observing thoughts and feelings, rather than being subsumed by them. So, instead of saying, "I'm useless," say, "I'm feeling useless right now." Instead of saying, "I ruined my chances," say, "I'm remembering a particularly painful memory right now." Put a discrete fence around the sensation, and you put limits on it and begin to understand that it is temporary. After all, how much of what we torment ourselves with is actually based in reality, and how much is simply *stories* we choose to tell ourselves?

It's great if you can put a little humor into it, too. When you can find humor, you can be resilient and somehow bigger than the big scary issue you're facing. Tell yourself, "Oh, here we go. My pity party is coming out in full force this afternoon," and try to find the absurdity in it all, imagining a little mini parade with tiny yet laughable balloons trotting out whenever you remember embarrassing events from your childhood. Poke fun at yourself—at the very least, know that you're definitely not the only one to harp on a bad memory.

Another thing to try is to deliberately ask yourself: **is what you're doing problem solving or rumination?** Be honest. On first chew, an idea might actually yield something useful or insightful. But generally, the more you go over an idea, the less you gain from it. We've seen that a powerful antidote to getting stuck in analysis mode is simply to act. Bring yourself into the concrete moment by actually *doing* something, rather than endlessly juggling potentials and guesses and worries.

If the answer is "I'm just ruminating," then force yourself to direct your attention to a single small action right now in the moment. Let's say you messed up and said something mean to a friend without thinking. You feel bad now. You replay the phrase in your head, cringing each time. Then you stop and ask, "Is what I'm doing problem solving or rumination?" You realize you're just chewing the psychological cud, and tell yourself to stop and instead think of a tiny thing you can do to improve the situation.

The problem is that you've offended your friend. The solution could be to apologize or reach out to mend the bridge. So do that. Think of it this way, if you're going to spend all the energy thinking over the problem, at least put it to good use and find a way to improve things. If you can't improve anything, then put your energy into distraction, forgiveness, or moving on.

By rechanneling anxious energy into things that will either improve your situation or at least help you come to terms with it, you are re-engaging with the world and getting out of the endless mental hurricane that goes nowhere but round and round in circles.

We've already spoken about distress tolerance, but you can go a long way to being mentally resilient simply by learning to distract yourself at the right moments. When you notice yourself ruminating ("Ah, here comes my rumination again. It's so boring with its same old stories . . ."), quickly throw yourself into an activity that absorbs all your attention. Get up and do thirty jumping jacks while saying the alphabet backward. Write out your shopping list for the week. Pick up your knitting, tidy your desk, or sing a complicated song, focusing intently on the lyrics. It doesn't really matter what you do, only that you temporarily break the rumination cycle by distracting yourself.

If you can't think of anything, focus on sensations from your five senses, or simply engage in physical activity, such as jogging or yoga. You don't have to stoically sit there and fight off intrusive thoughts—get up and literally shake them off if you like. If you hear your brain dipping into those "would have, should have, could have, what if, maybe" style thoughts, jump in and nip it in the bud. Usually, we want to avoid getting distracted. But distraction can be a powerful tool if we use it consciously and with purpose.

Are you stewing over something you have zero control over?

Are you making a mountain out of a molehill?

Is your rumination doing anything at all to advance the situation or fix the problem?

Have you got any reason to believe that the story you're telling or your interpretation of events is all that great—i.e. should you even take your word for it?

Gain psychological distance by imagining that your rumination is a boring old friend who's always rabbiting on about something. Picture yourself in the position of a calm, impartial observer who knows deep down that the story is just that—a story. So, the boring old friend comes to you and says, "Remember that time a few years ago when you said you knew how to speak French and then someone spoke French to you and you had no idea how to respond? Remember that? That was so humiliating, right?"

Maybe you were triggered into this memory by seeing something on a TV show or recently met a friend who was there when the incident happened. In whatever way the rumination was triggered, though, once you are aware of it, you have two choices. You can join in with the friend and have a good, long, angsty discussion about how cringe-worthy the whole episode was and how much you suck as a person for telling such a stupid lie. *Or*, you could calmly tell the rumination, "Ah, yes, I know this old yarn. But that's in the past now. I learned my lesson and don't do that kind of thing to big myself up anymore, and people have long since forgotten my gaffe. Now, let me return to what I was doing . . ."

When the boring rumination friend pipes up again and invites you to replay the embarrassing scene, you respond with, "Hey, rumination, do you have anything new to say? Do you have any fresh ideas for practical steps I can take right now? If not, then goodbye. I'm busy with something else." Your mind is like Teflon. Easy. The rumination, a little disappointed that nobody is listening, wanders off.

Summary

- Now that we've identified what overthinking is, we need to know how to combat it. There are many things you can do to de-stress and calm an anxious, overthinking mind that are simple yet effective.
- The first thing you need to remember is a mantra called the four A's of stress management. These are avoid, alter, accept, and adapt. Avoiding things entails simply walking away from things you can't control. Some things are

simply not worth the effort and are best removed from our environments altogether. However, if we can't avoid it, we must learn how to alter our environment to remove the stressor. If we can't alter our environment, we have no choice but to accept it. Lastly, if we can't do much about the situation at all, we must adapt to it and learn how to cope with our stressor and reduce its damaging potential to a minimum.

- Another popular technique is journaling. When we overthink, we have tons of different thoughts swirling in our mind, which can feel overwhelming. However, when we write these down systematically, we can analyze them and evaluate whether these thoughts are merited at all. To build the habit, you can carry a pocket journal with you around and write whenever you feel it's necessary.

- A third technique we have is called the 5-4-3-2-1 technique. This is highly effective at stemming panic attacks, and it does so by involving all five of our senses. So, whenever you feel panic overcoming you, look for five things around you that you can see, four things you can touch, three that you can smell, two that you can hear, and one that you can taste. Engaging your senses distracts your brain from the overthinking.

- Rumination is anxious, unproductive overthinking. Like other types of anxiety, it can be addressed with awareness and psychological distance. Label thoughts as thoughts and personify or externalize old stories, and get into the habit of asking whether what you're doing is genuine problem solving or just rumination.

CHAPTER 2. KEEPING COOL, CALM, AND COLLECTED

- Tackling anxiety comes down to the learned skill of emotional regulation. Rather than deny or squash down our natural emotions, we learn to *manage* them consciously and deliberately. We do this by becoming **responsive** rather than **reactive**.
- Becoming responsive is about pausing before we act in a situation, practicing impulse control, looking at our own motivations, beliefs, and thoughts, and finding healthy solutions to problems that go beyond anxious overthinking.
- One way to be more responsive is to dissect situations in the ABC framework—antecedent, behavior, and consequence. We need to examine what precedes and what follows anxious behavior, and then work around it.

Building self-awareness of your habitual patterns takes time and is seldom caught in the heat of the moment. But by engineering our triggers and outcomes, we can take control of our anxious behavior and change it.

- Emotional dashboarding is a similar approach designed to introduce more conscious awareness and reduce reactivity.
- We carefully analyze the factual situation, our emerging thoughts and beliefs in that situation, our resulting emotions, our physical sensations, and the impulses or actions that all of this inspires (i.e. anxious overthinking). When we are aware of all the precipitating factors, we can step in and avert falling into the anxiety spiral.
- Worry postponement is a very direct and effective way of interrupting anxiety spirals. When you recognize yourself beginning to feel anxious, deliberately schedule a discrete time in the future to worry instead, and then continually bring your mind to the present. We can seldom eliminate worry from our lives,

but we *can* consciously limit its time of onset and the duration.

- Finally, the five whys is a method that can help you put definite and useful shape to vague worries and overanalysis. If you're dealing with a real problem or crisis, the five whys can help. Define the problem and then ask what caused it—repeating the why question five times to arrive at the real root cause, which you can then act on.

- Avoid this method if your anxieties are not attached to any real dilemma or decision. The questions are designed to elevate overthinking into clarity and problem solving—not more overthinking!

CHAPTER 3. DEBUGGING THE MACHINE

- Uncertainty, discomfort, and negative emotions are a part of life, and sometimes anxiety is unavoidable, but we can "debug the machine" that is our brain and choose to adopt a mindset that works for us.

- Distress tolerance means accepting that distress is part of life, but also knowing that we can endure it and thrive regardless. We can identify triggers and warning signs, and then deliberately choose not to escape into overthinking, avoidance, or self-soothing behaviors, but sit with our distress. By accepting our feelings, we minimize the power anxiety has over us, and teach ourselves that we are competent to withstand what life throws our way.

- Detachment comes from Buddhist theory or the writing of the ancient Stoics. In their respective ways, they teach us to build inner resilience. Pain is inevitable, but in attaching to it, we cause suffering, which is a choice. We can decide to cultivate emotional serenity and equanimity. With conscious awareness, we can break our attachment and simply accept reality for what it is.

- Neutrality is the commitment to facing life as it is, and realizing that events are neutral, and it is our mental and emotional interpretation that decides whether they are good or bad. Outside forces do not make us anxious, rather our own thoughts and beliefs do, and we have control over those. Realizing this, we understand that we have the power to create our reality.

- Gratitude and the ability to savor life pulls us out of anxious rumination and overthinking and counteracts our natural bias for the negative. By dwelling on the good things in life, we remind ourselves of our blessings, foster positive emotions, and counteract negativity.

- We can use CBT to unpick the negative and unhelpful thoughts and feelings we have about reality with neutrality and awareness. We can observe our thoughts, challenge them (they are not the same as reality!), and then replace them with something deliberately more adaptive and realistic.

- We can **train** our attention, rather than letting it run wild, dragging our wellbeing with it. We can do this by focusing our five senses on a mundane task and bringing our awareness back to the simple present.

- Meditation is the deliberate and consistent cultivation of awareness, focus, and relaxation.
- Some widespread notions about meditation are nothing but myths. You don't need to convert to Buddhism or even incorporate religious elements in your practice. Meditation is not selfish avoidance of reality; rather, it cultivates full acceptance of reality. Meditation also does not require fighting with yourself just to keep your mind clear.
- While mindfulness is generally taken to be a state that can be fostered through the practice of meditation, some people consider mindfulness as itself a form of meditation, along with other forms such as yoga, tantra, and visualization.
- There are many different types of meditation, and you can practice the one you resonate most with. Guided meditation involves a recorded voice or live teacher leading a structured meditation session. Loving-kindness

meditation trains you to yield your conscious awareness toward developing self-compassion. Mantra meditation has you speak out a repeated or meaningless word or sound to anchor you in the present. In breathing meditation, you focus on your breath in order to stay in the moment. Mindfulness meditation involves a conscious practice of nonjudgment and non-attachment while cultivating awareness of the present.

- It's best to have a routine as to when and where you meditate. Choose a time and place where you're relatively free from distractions. Most important is that your practice is consistent and that you approach it with a willingness to meet each moment with calm, kind awareness.

- Among the most common challenges in meditation are lack of consistency; expecting too much; impatience; low self-esteem and doubt; and an out-of-control, racing mind resulting from a highly stimulating day with a lot of stresses and unhealthy habits.

- It will take time to make meditation a habit, but you can help it along by attaching it to other daily habits you already have. Habit anchoring, a technique wherein you designate a thirty-second activity as a prompt for your meditation practice, helps you incorporate meditation more easily in your daily life. You can also employ the habit loop formula, which consists of a cue, a reward, and a craving as elements of establishing a new routine.

CHAPTER 5. DE-STRESS FOR A NEW YOU

- Now that we've identified what overthinking is, we need to know how to combat it. There are many things you can do to de-stress and calm an anxious, overthinking mind that are simple yet effective.
- The first thing you need to remember is a mantra called the four A's of stress management. These are avoid, alter, accept, and adapt. Avoiding things entails simply walking away from things you can't control. Some things are simply not worth the effort and are best

removed from our environments altogether. However, if we can't avoid it, we must learn how to alter our environment to remove the stressor. If we can't alter our environment, we have no choice but to accept it. Lastly, if we can't do much about the situation at all, we must adapt to it and learn how to cope with our stressor and reduce its damaging potential to a minimum.

- Another popular technique is journaling. When we overthink, we have tons of different thoughts swirling in our mind, which can feel overwhelming. However, when we write these down systematically, we can analyze them and evaluate whether these thoughts are merited at all. To build the habit, you can carry a pocket journal with you around and write whenever you feel it's necessary.

- A third technique we have is called the 5-4-3-2-1 technique. This is highly effective at stemming panic attacks, and it does so by involving all five of our senses. So, whenever you feel panic overcoming you, look for five things around you that you can see, four things you can touch, three that you can smell, two that you can hear, and one that you can taste. Engaging your senses distracts your brain from the overthinking.

- Rumination is anxious, unproductive overthinking. Like other types of anxiety, it can be addressed with awareness and psychological distance. Label thoughts as thoughts and personify or externalize old stories, and get into the habit of asking whether what you're doing is genuine problem solving or just rumination.

9 781647 433000